99039

Crean, S. M., 1945-
    Two nations : an essay on the culture and
politics of Canada and Quebec in a world
of American pre-eminence / Susan Crean and
Marcel Rioux. Toronto : Lorimer, c1983.
    167 p.
    Translated from the French.

1. Canada - Civilization - American
influences.
(Continued on next card)
0888623828   1983180 NLC
088862381X pb   1983199
                                    6/CC

Two
Nations

An essay on the culture and politics
of Canada and Quebec in a world
of American pre-eminence

Two Nations

Susan Crean and Marcel Rioux

James Lorimer & Company, Publishers

Toronto 1983

ISBN 0-88862-381-X paper
      0-88862-382-8 cloth

Design: Laurel Angeloff

Author photos: Jerry Grey (Susan Crean),
                La Presse (Marcel Rioux)

Canadian Cataloguing in Publication Data

Crean, S.M., 1945–
    Two nations

English version of: Deux pays pour vivre.
Authors' names in reverse order on French ed.
1. Canada—Civilization—American influences.
2. Canada—English-French relations.*   3. Quebec
(Province)—History—Autonomy and independence
movements.   4. Canada—Relations—United States.
5. United States—Relations—Canada.   I. Rioux, Marcel,
1919–   II. Title.

FC97.R513 1983   917.064   C83-098859-9
F1027.R513 1983

The authors wish to acknowledge the support of the Canada Council and the Ontario Arts Council.

James Lorimer & Company, Publishers
Egerton Ryerson Memorial Building
35 Britain Street
Toronto, Ontario M5A 1R7

Printed and bound in Canada

6 5 4 3 2 1   83 84 85 86 87 88

Contents

Two nations; between whom there is not intercourse and no sympathy; who are as ignorant of each other's habits, thoughts and feelings as if they were dwellers in different zones, or inhabitants of different planets; who are formed by a different breeding, are fed by different food and are ordered by different manners and are not governed by the same laws. —
THE RICH AND THE POOR.

Benjamin Disraeli

Introduction

Susan Crean

There is a well-known saying, often heard in Quebec, that the more things change, the more they stay the same: *Plus ça change, plus c'est la même chose.* In the whirl of current events, rising unemployment and falling dollars, the sensation of change can be compelling but is in a certain sense illusory. For all the combined zeal and imagination of the various reform movements of the Sixties, neither Mohammed nor the mountain has budged very far. In Canada, too, those who have toiled in the vineyards for social reform have learned how hardy the resistance to change is. What we cannot be certain about yet is whether Canadians and Quebeckers will go on as before, following the lead of those who already possess power and prestige (and have no reason to relinquish it), looking to an exhausted leadership, its imagination spent, for inspiration and solutions that will never come.

The thoughts we explore in this book are addressed not to our political and economic élites but to the general public—Canadians and Quebeckers together. Despite a new constitution, the old problems still haunt us; as predicted, the 1980 referendum on sovereignty–association resolved none of the fundamental questions raised by the *indépendantistes* in Quebec, and sooner or later, we believe, it will be necessary for Canadians and Quebeckers to sit down together to work out a new type of association.

Perhaps it was reasonable for the partisans of sovereignty-association to confine their energies to convincing Quebeckers, but they have still an unfinished task convincing us all that a new arrangement could be the best chance for both nations to save and safeguard themselves as distinct societies. Such is the thesis Marcel Rioux and I present in this book. We are both profoundly attached to our nations, but at the same time we hope that the two will someday reach an understanding that will permit them to fulfil the promise with which they have been endowed by history.

Our arguments, therefore, try to go beyond our particular situation in North America and assert that our destiny is linked to the destiny of other nations, which are also subject to the cultural and economic pressures of the American empire. Because Canada and Quebec happen to border the United States and because we are often cited as prime examples of advanced Americanization, we feel we have a special responsibility to ourselves and to the world community to face this situation critically and try to regain our autonomy.

It is uncommon in our history for a Quebecker and a Canadian to collaborate in writing and publishing their joint reflections — especially an *indépendantiste* and a nationalist. So it may be useful to describe how this book came to be.

In the summer of 1977, at a meeting arranged by the Canada Council at Stanley House in the Gaspésie, we had occasion, Marcel Rioux and I, to exchange ideas and talk about our two nations at length. We became aware then that from two very opposite points of personal and intellectual departure we had arrived at very similar conclusions. We found ourselves in agreement on many levels and on many essentials and therefore decided to carry on the dialogue. Eventually we resolved to be more systematic and to put our reflections on paper. But so that each of us would have the freedom to write from a particular cultural perspective, we conceived the idea of co-authoring two books at once. Marcel Rioux would write the volume in French for Quebec readers, with my assistance, and I would write the version in English, with his. If these books demonstrate anything, it must be that great differences — in our case the divergence of religion, class and educational background as well as of language, sex and generation — need not be obstacles to understanding, but can be the basis for a true and sympathetic friendship. It was certainly so for Rioux and me.

If over the years Canadians and Quebeckers have emphasized and liberally expounded on their differences, there has been very little effort on either side to explore their similarities or to illuminate shared experience. At the most fundamental level, what Rioux and I discovered we do share is our feeling of attachment to our people and place — what used to be called patriotism, that deep caring for one's country and compatriots that goes hand in hand with an acceptance and respect for other nations. We also found that we had come separately to similar conclusions about the health of our respective cultures, believing them to be mortally threatened by the same combination of industrial and ideological forces, wrought within and beyond our borders. We are convinced that cultural domination has become the supreme form of imperialism in our age, and we feel that failure to acknowledge this paves the way for all sorts of pedestrian oppression. In sensing this, moreover, we have both had to defy the convention that localizes and trivializes the cultural side of life, removing it from the main arena where only economics and politics are supposed to hold sway. So, in arguing for the national autonomy of Canada and Quebec, we adopt a global perspective, as citizens living in the top half of North America.

In certain circles it is *de rigueur* to scoff at those who talk of breaking out of political and economic dependence because, the sceptics say, we are living in an era of grandiose scale, of transnational corporations and global interdependencies, meaning that we have to rely on the vast economic and technical networks already in place just to keep up. They say there is no choice if we are going to keep up our GNP. Yet ordinary people have begun to ask themselves whether corporations and governments, the legions of modern-day empire, are designed to satisfy the needs of people or their own needs. The plethora of "needs" so diligently serviced by these mastodons also sustains their power and, it turns out, robs individuals and groups of their knowledge, skills and values in the process. Far from being a backward move, it seems to us that winning national autonomy would be a positive and propitious step and one that would flow from the new awareness and changed perspectives fostered by dissent.

Because our plea for Canada and Quebec is above all made on cultural grounds, we are not interested in what social scientists call "normal." The notion of normality, applied to individuals or human groups, contains the hint of conformity, as defined by statistics or as codified into social custom. We should remember, though, that science has shown there are some organisms in nature that, by adapting themselves to a contracted and externally controlled environment, can still be considered normal from the point of view of the ecosystem as a whole. So, too, human beings can adapt themselves to life in reduced and deviant circumstances. Yet only humans have the ability to invent new values and structures in the face of a restrictive or debilitating situation. This is the essence of "normative" being—the individual who refuses to be normal, to be distorted by events and circumstances, and who demands instead that *they* be changed. What applies to individuals also applies to collectivities.

To follow the process, however, we have to begin with personal experience and find in our own pasts the illustration of the abstract and theoretical topics we discuss in this book. Far from proposing ourselves as models of anything, we only wish to show how we all, within our different milieux, have the opportunity to observe some inconsistencies and the hardships handed some and not others by society. We can say, perhaps with a touch of modesty, that in our own cases, Rioux's and mine, disowning these contradictions and questioning received truth began a journey from adolescent disbelief and scepticism about convention to open dissent and an ultimate break with a traditional set of values. So, too, our philosophic peregrinations took us in the same direction, from the personal and particular to the general and political. In our own histories, then, we can perceive that there is a dialectic at work that comprises rupture and renewal, rejection and acceptance, endings and beginnings, like life itself. As André Gide once said, there comes a time in life when one has to review all one's allegiances.

Marcel Rioux is a Québécois of peasant stock, descendant of farmers and rural folk who for three hundred years or so have worked and lived out their lives in the beautiful Bas-du-Fleuve country, in the heart of the Gaspé peninsula. Catholic and French-speaking, his family was nurtured in a traditional Québécois village society. They knew neither affluence nor privilege beyond the modest reward of hard work and stout allegiance to the Church and community. The Church was, of course, the all-pervasive fact of life, at home and at school; but if its influence was everywhere evident, so was the hypocrisy that accepted worldly sin and corruption among the clergy so long as there was no public scandal. Even to a thirteen-year-old boy, the message was crystal-clear: it was not mandatory to believe, so long as one conformed. At school this meant making deals, often unspoken deals, with the priests in charge;

misbehaviour would be tolerated on both sides if it were kept under wraps, if dissent and deviance were hidden. This did not mean that Rioux's questioning of religious authority stopped. Eventually the discrepancy between its teachings and practice led to his first major rupture. Upon graduation, Rioux left home and the Gaspé and at the same time abandoned religion for good. Turning to the study of anthropology and philosophy, including socialist thought, he discovered new ways of looking at human society.

For Marcel Rioux, as for many of us, the rejection of certain ideas and values accompanied by a judgment of the political role of the groups promulgating them was experienced at first on a personal level. But this in itself is not enough to explain the fact that some individuals go on to rebel against accepted order while others settle down and submit to it.

Beyond purely individual factors, can we detect any common social phenomena that account for such ruptures? Certainly, all societies act through the ideological apparatus, such as the family and the education system, to reproduce and perpetuate their structures and cultures. In traditional societies, which tend to be uniform and conformist and which can operate on a massive consensus, social revolt is rare. In our pluralistic society, however, delinquents and deviants are as common as crabgrass. The distinction between the two is important: the delinquent rejects the means sanctioned by society for gaining certain ends, while the deviant rejects the assumptions and even the values of established authority. The delinquent defies the rules of the game, usually for immediate and personal gain; the deviant's objective may well be to rewrite the rules entirely. Whatever tag they are given, society has always considered social reformers more dangerous than delinquents precisely because reformers question society's very legitimacy. But in contemporary liberal societies, the control of deviance is exercised more by ideological than by physical inhibition.

We are thinking here particularly of the effects of cultural domination and of our own experience in Canada and Quebec with the influence of American culture. Since this book is about domination and dependence, we are bound to ask whether the repudiation of American domination is not connected to larger issues. Perhaps, on the other hand, it is possible for individuals to conform for the most part while taking issue with, say, economic or cultural domination.

It seems to us that there are two hypotheses. Some

Quebeckers, for instance, are nationalists because they want to take over the positions occupied by the English-Canadian élites. And some Canadians are nationalists because of a parallel aspiration to replace the Americans. Neither group questions the make-up of society or the apportionment of power. Nationalism or, in this case, national liberation is simply a means of acquiring privilege by unseating and replacing a foreign élite.

At the other extreme are the disinherited and disadvantaged, who revolt against the ruling order, whatever it may be, to redress injustice and improve their lot in life. However, neither hypothesis explains a rebel like Rioux, an individual who managed through education to escape the confines of a hard background and achieve a comfortable life. One common explanation is that such rebels are deluded malcontents who only want to lay waste to society, to replace order with disorder. They are characterized as misguided idealists and selfish dreamers pursuing their own lovely vision of utopia, oblivious to the misery they cause.

We would not deny that malice and recklessness exist, but there is in the human make-up an instinct to build as well as to destroy, and it seems to us that the two go together. Institutions no less than buildings may have to be dismantled in order for them to be rebuilt.

Whether the process is peaceful or violent, one element is always there: the creative imagination. The desire to bring about a freer, less alienating society has inspired many actions, but the ability to imagine such a society to begin with, and then to see how it can emerge out of the present, must be there first. It is this that gives meaning to the slogan scribbled on Paris walls by the revolutionaries in May 1968: *Prenez vos rêves pour la réalité* — "Take your dreams for reality."

Rioux and I believe that national autonomy is a necessary condition for the realization of other forms of individual and collective autonomy. It may also prove to be true that national liberation can only be reached as part of a sequence of liberations occurring in several domains, emancipation in one area a kind of apprenticeship for the next. This was the way we two came to be nationalists. In Rioux's case, disillusionment with the Church went along with the denunciation of its collusion with the quasi-fascist Duplessis regime and an awareness of the injustices of social class. Two events in the late Forties, the Asbestos strike and the publication of Paul-Émile Borduas's *Refus Global*, crystallized the conflicts.

Quebec would have to rid itself of both Duplessis and the pernicious influence of the Church in civil society. This was the project that united a disparate band of reformers for a decade, triumphing in the election of Jean Lesage and the provincial Liberals in 1960.

It was in the late Forties, in the Paris of Léon Blum and Jean-Paul Sartre, that Rioux became a socialist; and it was there also that he was introduced to the life of the intellectual man-of-action—the *engagé*. He had by this time already turned his attention as an anthropologist to studying Quebec society, and on returning home he immediately became involved in political and cultural groups advancing secular, socialist and nationalist approaches to Quebec's problems.

At a different time and by different routes, this was my itinerary, too, only I began the journey with the women's movement. For both of us, the culmination of the progression was the unveiling of the colonial reality. It seems to us, therefore, that national autonomy must rightly involve social and cultural considerations as well as political and economic ones, and that liberation in these areas is necessary for a self-determining society where women and men can work in full equality and creativity.

It was the American psychologist Erich Fromm who named that most peculiar of contemporary human maladies the "escape from freedom," whereby people invent ways to justify a state of dependence and inure themselves to it. We are well cared for by our society; the United States is there to defend us against the Russians, and the Canadian government is here to alleviate egregious social injustice. We do not have to shoulder responsibility for much of anything. Caring for the old, teaching children, healing the sick and burying the dead—there is always a specialist around to take over and do the job for us.

We believe this attitude, and this way of doing things, has been the undoing of Western civilization. If it is radical to trace such issues and problems back to their roots, and to push their implications to their global conclusions, then the reader will find our reflections radical. In our opinion, however, the times demand it. We will need imagination and largeness of spirit to escape both the clichés of thought and rhetoric and our own acquired interests and attachments to social class. So many barriers have been erected between Canada and Quebec—between the peoples of our two nations—that it is probably necessary to strip back our relationship to its essentials in order to envision other possibilities. But because we know in our hearts and from experience that Canada and Quebec are distinct nations (which is not to say "nation-states"), we tend through this book to identify them that way. However, at times, especially when speaking historically, we revert to the traditional terms, Quebec being part of a larger entity called Canada. Context should guide the reader through these shifting connotations.

We begin in Chapter 1 with a look at the relationship between Canada and Quebec, now that the referendum is over and the Constitution home, considering the achievements of nationalist movements over the past two decades. Chapter 2 reviews the blotted history of Canada–US relations, exploring the economic and cultural conditions of life here in the colonies. Expanding on this, Chapter 3 turns to the question of America's global pre-eminence and how it holds other countries in thrall, tied to a network of ever-deepening military and economic interdependence. Can national cultures survive the power and allure of American technology? Are sovereignty and self-determination utopian ideals? Will Soviet-style Communism and American-style capitalism find a way to make peace and save the planet? In Chapter 4 we argue that in turning from the inevitability of nuclear war and/or ecological and economic catastrophe, we will find in the human imagination endless possibilities for reinventing our destiny, beginning with self-determination. We have to begin with ourselves and our society — with Canada and Quebec.

Finally, we hope this book will contribute to the debate about how we can turn the future to the individual and collective advantage of the people living here, taking back the knowledge, skills and powers delegated for so long to others. In turning back the tide of American empire, Canada and Quebec have common cause. The dream Rioux and I have is that through such an understanding, we will be able to create a new association.

Toronto
June 1983

Chapter 1
Deux Pays pour Vivre

Never in our history have there been so many agonizing questions raised about the nature and health of society as there have been over the past twenty years. Doubts have been expressed about the most fundamental social arrangements; accusations of injustice have been levelled at old, respectable institutions; and some people truly believe that this *fin de siècle* will be the last one for humanity and possibly for all things living on this planet. Not since ancient times have there been so many soothsayers and prophets milling about the market-place, selling their visions of the future. And not since the dawn of modern times has the future seemed so unpredictable.

In essence the questions have been of two varieties: those concerning the character and constitution of industrially advanced society in the late twentieth century, and those concerning the character and constitution of Canada in particular. We propose to deal with both, because each affects the other. One cannot, for instance, take issue with the economic and cultural influence of the United States in this country without criticizing the type of society that engenders and approves of such domination. By the same token, if Canadians and Quebeckers talk about regaining their independence, surely it is not for the purpose of perpetuating an outworn order, but to do something different.

What then does independence mean? For a nation-state, it

means having political sovereignty, which is to say, the supreme and final power to direct its own affairs. In both Quebec and Canada, it can be equated with the desire to take control of major decisions affecting the life of the nation, its citizens and their institutions. Yet this obviously implies something deeper; for if the group of individuals composing the nation attach a value to their right to self-determination, it must be because they believe they have a future together and want (as the historians say) to accomplish great things together. The motivation for as yet unrealized independence arises first from dissatisfaction with the existing state of affairs, then coalesces around the search for more consonant priorities and directions. In substance, it is the expressed desire of a society to create itself out of its own history and on its own terms — and in so doing, to invent something different. We imagine ourselves, therefore we make the means to be.

For many years now, but especially since the Parti Québécois came to power in 1976, the Quebec question has been a national obsession. The subject has been worked over by so many committees, commissions, politicians and editorialists that it seems futile to try adding anything to the discussion. Furthermore, many Canadians are under the impression that the 1980 referendum settled it once and for all. By contrast, the Americanization of the Canadian and Québécois communities has been touched on so superficially and fleetingly that you might think it an embarrassing family secret. Governments on both sides of the Ottawa River behave as if Canada and Quebec occupied the North American continent alone. Yet our relationship to the United States is a key piece in the puzzle, and obviously no one can hope to change any part of the picture without first looking at it in its entirety.

Perhaps now that Quebec's not-so-Quiet Revolution is over twenty-one, we have the perspective for useful reflection; have the actions and ideas of Québécois nationalists availed us? In the past two decades there has been a burst of creative activity, born of a new maturity and determination that led many people to wonder aloud about collective identity and national survival. The ruminations quickly acquired a political voice, followed by demands for radical change. Quebeckers have always distrusted the centralization of economic and political power in Ottawa, and the lesson of the Act of Union and Confederation is well understood. To this day Quebeckers and political parties of all colours are prepared to defend themselves on this battlefield, though many consider it futile. The constitutional "accord" of November 1981, which saw Quebec isolated and deliberately left out of the agreement made by the nine English-Canadian provinces, is only the most recent demonstration of that historical reality: when the interests of the French-speaking minority do not coincide with those of the English-speaking majority, English Canada will rule.

Through the Sixties and Seventies a growing number of Quebeckers came to the conclusion that, at least in Quebec, that rule should change. In 1979, the Parti Québécois advanced a concrete proposal and called for a referendum on it. Specifically, the PQ suggested that Quebec should assert its sovereignty, with all the political powers necessary to assure its social and cultural integrity, and then negotiate a new economic association with Canada, equal to equal. The 1980 referendum asked Quebeckers to grant the government the power to begin negotiations.

Curiously, English Canadians in Canada and in Quebec reacted every bit as emotionally as did French-speaking Quebeckers to the PQ's proposal. Economist Abraham Rotstein has described English Canada's brand of nationalism as "mappism," a kind of exaggerated identification of the nation with its territory. For many English Canadians, the association proposed by the Parti Québécois threatened to punch a yawning gap in that integral expanse of land stretching from sea to sea. Since so much of the Canadian economic and cultural enterprise had already been given away to the Americans (including the mineral wealth beneath the map's surface), it could be that on a subconscious level Canadians do perceive territory as the one tangible element of the nation left inviolate. Certainly the impending "break-up" of the nation was almost physically felt. Quebec became a national crisis.

From the beginning, the response of English Canada to Quebec's constitutional challenge has been monopolized by those most in league with the *status quo*: businessmen and politicians. Given the close associations among these men of power, and the ease with which they travel back and forth from one milieu to the other, we can understand why a certain level of regionalist dissent can be tolerated and can work to their advantage. If the voices of change and protest are divided, if region can be pitted against region, it is easier to maintain power at the centre.

In the aftermath of 1976, the government in Ottawa

appointed a task force to investigate Canadian unity and put two grandfatherly figures in charge, the retired premier of Ontario, John Robarts, and the former federal minister of industry, trade and commerce, Jean-Luc Pepin. The Pepin-Robarts committee in its report opted for an idealized version of the Balkan states, where every province becomes a self-centred little tin-pot republic. What better vision of the glories in that future than the attitudes (and infighting) of recent Western separatist parties. By treating regionalism as a one-dimensional political term and insisting on a geographical definition, the Pepin-Robarts report gave the impression that regional identity is more or less the antithesis of national identity, so that strengthening one comes only at the expense of the other. (More power to the province means less power for Ottawa.) That impression seems to be substantiated by the feeble attempts of Liberal governments over the years to concoct a national identity out of the bland bilingual, multicultural pablum it serves up on Canada Day. Such processed unity may fit a political idea of the country (two languages, many cultures), but it denies the existence of our two national societies and trivializes the authentic regional divergences in our cultures.

The ingenuity of the Pepin-Robarts report was in nationalizing regionalism, as Mel Watkins put it, and in promoting it as the solution to Quebec's demands. The Quebec Liberal party's counter-proposal to sovereignty–association adopted the same formula. The so-called Beige Paper was the brainchild of Claude Ryan, the intellectually authoritative and revered former editor of *Le Devoir* who was drafted to the Liberal leadership by those who saw him as federalism's last hope in Quebec and the only man who could fell Lévesque. Ryan's proposal, *A New Canadian Confederation*, called for a reformed Senate and greatly expanded provincial rights in which Quebec would in essence have special status. Both these proposals take the semantic approach: Quebec is a region (like any other), and all the regions can have special status if they want it. Instead of encouraging an awakening of English Canada's own national sensibility, which might help Canadians respond to Quebec with equal confidence and self-knowledge, Pepin-Robarts retreated to constitutional high ground, absolving itself with the excuse that it is easier to change the constitution than to foster unity among Canadians! The assumption seems to have been that the proper constitution would magically produce that elusive unity.

The Pepin-Robarts report and Ryan's Beige Paper were both quickly bypassed by events and soon forgotten. But once the referendum was "won" by the federalist forces, Trudeau resurrected his own project for constitutional reform. His move to carry this out without provincial ratification was challenged in the Supreme Court; and the decision that held that the prime minister's plan accorded with the BNA Act pointed out that it was not in accord with convention. Patriation—as the complete process of amending the act, bringing it home to Canada and appending a charter of rights was tagged—went ahead as planned. Predictably this took us on a tortuous ride through labyrinths of legalese and a public debate that centred mainly on the charter. Here native groups and women—two rather important "minorities"—had to marshal their forces, arguing before Commons committees and the British parliament just to have their basic rights guaranteed.

Of course, retrieving the constitution from England and sprucing it up with a new charter of rights did nothing to change the mechanics of Confederation. The inequities persist. Since 1980 Westerners have become as outspoken as Quebeckers in their vilification of Ottawa and all it stands for—above all, for their effective disenfranchisement. There is virulent resentment of Ottawa and the Liberal regime abroad in the land, undiminished by the Tory interregnum. In Quebec, independence is as live an issue as ever; the referendum, in that sense, settled nothing. As the pundits said at the time, either a "yes" or a "no" vote was a vote for some serious change. The night of the referendum, thousands of "yes" supporters crowded into Paul Sauvé arena, singing, weeping and cheering René Lévesque as he conceded defeat. Quebeckers, he said, wanted to give federalism a last chance; the ball had been returned to Ottawa's court, but the game was far from over. One year later, the PQ was re-elected with more seats than before, and soon there were several strategies being discussed within the party: running candidates federally, fighting the next provincial election on sovereignty. Meanwhile militants inside and outside the PQ who have had enough of the *étapiste*, go-slow approach to independence are reassessing the party's record in power, and particularly its handling of public-sector labour relations.

Understandably, the association part of sovereignty-association has fallen by the wayside. In Quebec, as in the rest of Canada, there are few people actively engaged in rethinking our relationship. In any case, in Quebec there is still assimilation to worry about, and the fact is that religion and language, the ancient ramparts of Quebec society, are no longer adequate defence. The history of French-Canadian nationalism is the history of a search for survival that eventually came to rest in the province of Quebec, and it is as a French-speaking, Quebec majority that French Canada is approaching English Canada today, equal to equal, not in such absolute terms as population but as one founding nation to another.

The PQ opened up one road, but failed to win a majority in the referendum. They did obtain a majority of French-speaking voters, but not a majority of French- and English-speaking voters combined. As a result, Ottawa assumed dominion over Canada–Quebec relations once again; the bureaucrats on both sides resumed their paper warfare, and Quebec disappeared from the headlines. Prime Minister Trudeau went back to insisting that all Quebeckers should feel at home everywhere in Canada, while every day, anglicization takes its toll of the French communities outside Quebec. For a brief moment it looked as if constitutional reform might reopen the debate on Canada's relationship with Quebec, at least within official circles. It didn't, and the issue lies dormant for the time being, waiting for another political crisis, another seizure in the body politic. We have all just lived through an extraordinary period of intense political activity, and there is widespread fatigue. Still, this could be the most opportune time to reflect on what we have achieved as two societies and where we might go from here. To do that we should begin by setting down a few propositions on which everyone can agree.

First, all attempts so far to assimilate Quebec within the Canadian nation (1840 and 1867 included) have failed. Quebec today is undeniably a distinct nation and, some would say, a credible economic and cultural entity. It is an entity, in any case, with growing aspirations for independence that produced a massive (forty per cent is significant by any standard) if not majority vote for sovereignty–association in 1980.

Second, a nationalist movement, expressed primarily in terms of economic nationalism, has taken root in Canada. So far it has gained little power, though it has had some popular influence. Because of it, the Liberal National Energy Program and the purchase of Petro-Canada were possible, even if they were no more than nationalist window-dressing by the Liberal government.

Third, the provinces of English Canada have taken to

airing their grievances against Ottawa's centralization and bemoaning their historic lot in Confederation. All of them are now interested in reforming the Senate and dividing power differently between Ottawa and the provinces.

Fourth, there is a growing awareness in both Canada and Quebec of American imperialism and its methods of economic and cultural domination around the world. For that matter, Americans are themselves more conscious and critical of their country's conduct abroad. And, along with everything else, this sensibility has spilled over into Canada with *The NBC Nightly News*.

Finally, the social protest movements of the Sixties and Seventies, which attacked a bewildering collection of issues and injustices—among them racial and sexual discrimination, war, pollution and the hazards of nuclear energy—were very pointed in their critique of the basic underpinnings of industrialized society. Even the most comfortable of Western nations underwent involuntary psychoanalysis administered by dissidents, reformers and student groups who questioned the wisdom, the competence, the motivation and indeed the world-view of the political, military and corporate establishment. Now, however, that the economy seems to be descending into a state of more or less permanent depression, other priorities impinge, and we are told that this is no time to daydream. So the social project has been abandoned. These days, everyone takes the fact of Americanization pretty much for granted. We know that it is there—that it is everywhere—narcotic, noxious even, but not, in the immediate scale of problems, critical.

The dumping of US culture has been seen by nationalists here chiefly as an obstacle to self-development and self-expression. But we in Canada are not the only ones to wonder whether we are suffering from over-exposure to the American dream. People everywhere are wondering. No matter where one stands in relation to the current Soviet–US shoving match, the global spread of America's mass communications system is being felt wherever people are striving for self-realization, democracy and independence.

The nation, as we talk of it here and throughout this book, refers to society as a collective unit. Historians and philosophers have gone to convoluted lengths to refine a definition of the nation, isolating factors such as shared language, history, race or territory. Any or all of these elements may or may not be present, and in varying degrees, in a given situation. However, there is one element, in many respects the most elusive, that is always there if a nation exists, and that is identity — the sense of a national community felt by individuals or members of a society. All the other outward and visible factors that have been included in the various and varied descriptions do not themselves guarantee that a nation will exist. And a group of people may well consider themselves to be a nation even if they do not at the time constitute a nation-state. Moreover, national groups, by accident of history, have often straddled political borders.

So it is national identity that, in the final analysis, determines the existence of a nation. Accordingly, the strength or weakness of this sentiment affects a society's ability to conduct its own affairs successfully, to plan projects, to organize institutions that will educate the new generation and to perpetuate itself.

What then is national identity and where does it come from? A nation, like an individual, constructs its identity through a process of identification and differentiation: identification with people and groups with whom one shares certain attributes or perspectives, and differentiation from others, perhaps nearby, who embody a different set of characteristics or who, in some fundamental way, behave differently. Concerning individual personality, identity is the answer to the question "Who am I?" or "Where do I belong?" It comes out in encounters with others that reveal similarities and differences in such a way that people can position themselves in relation to others in the social web. So, too, the national community defines itself by distinguishing between "us" and "them."

The process is dynamic as individuals and communities are perpetually modifying and being modified by events and experience. Out of it, however, comes the sense of communality that draws people together and kindles their desire to undertake social projects. Here is the point of origin of Rousseau's social contract, where social consensus is built and the collective dream dreamt. Notwithstanding the size and importance in daily life of those institutions created by the social contract (whether it be the public transit system or the institution of marriage), they usually help shape our perception and expectations for society. It is the *esprit de corps* that matters, the spirit that underlies all social structures and inspires individuals with a sense of belonging. It is this experience of nationhood that ultimately creates the nation.

By this definition, we can see that unlike the nation-state, which tends to be unitary and monolithic, national identity is multifarious. All societies are more or less pluralistic and display their own patchworks of minorities and subcultures. To the individual, national identity is manifest as part of a whole range of ideas and experiences, not as a single phenomenon. It is one link in a chain of identities making up the human personality. For we are all members of many communities—the family, the neighbourhood, the club, the office, the profession and so forth. Of course, nations can be stereotyped and usually are by outsiders. Mistaking this simplistic, shorthand characterization for the essence of national identity, many Canadians have wandered off into the wilderness like sasquatch hunters questing a mythological beast. If American-ness can be equated with apple pie, what's the quintessential Canadian expression? (When CBC's *This Country in the Morning* ran a contest to fill in the blank in "As Canadian as . . .," the winning answer was "As Canadian as possible under the circumstances," which could just be as accurate as it is cynical.)

As we have tried to suggest, identification and differentiation are complementary opposites, like two co-ordinates fixing a position. Where individuals or groups are concerned, however, distortions in the process do occur. We know that people can suffer from a variety of identity crises and complexes. So do nations. An inferiority complex in a nation, for instance, may manifest itself as a colonial mentality, an excess of identification with a foreign culture and a repressed sense of one's own. This could be the first step to assimilation—the blurring of psychological boundaries. At the other extreme, such complexes in nations can produce bigotry, discrimination, even persecution.

We do not, of course, propose to offer a *carte blanche* defence of any and all forms of nationalism. To argue, however, as does Trudeau, that we should lead the world into some kind of ethnic nirvana by renouncing nationalism altogether is equally absurd. A sick nation like Nazi Germany offers one example of how national feeling can be exploited as an instrument of class and race oppression. But having said that, we must also acknowledge the importance of British and Russian patriotism in defeating the Third Reich. The point, surely, is that nationalism is by definition neither good nor bad, though it most certainly can be applied to either end. Nor are nationalist policies necessarily extremist (and here we have to distinguish between the nationalism that is the spirit and identity of a people and nationalism as practised by the state). Nevertheless, the most evil and violent forms of state nationalism have tarred all nationalism with the same brush, giving the proponents of continental integration and federalism occasion to discredit the quite legitimate aims and concerns of nationalists in Quebec and Canada.

What we are saying is that nationalism is part of the human make-up and a concrete fact of human society. It is natural and entirely desirable for governments to take the part of their citizens, looking to their welfare and rights in particular. It is natural in the sense that such action accords with the principles of responsibility and self-realization and ought to be the outgrowth of democracy. What we should fear is any state or class that tries to extend its rule over others, bending their needs and desires to its interests.

In an age of proliferating nation-states, the relationship between peoples and governments has special importance. For the United Nations and the diplomatic community, recognition of new countries is a ticklish political matter that is usually dealt with on the legal and political plane rather than the social or cultural level. Hence we have had oddities such as Taiwan's prolonged career as a permanent member of the Security Council and as the only representative of nearly a billion Chinese. Although it is probably reasonable to treat governments as the embodiment of their nations abroad, at home they are, of course, just one aspect of all that makes up national life. It is also true that governments, whether self-appointed or elected, generally represent not the whole of a society but some part of it—a political party, a social class, an ethnic or religious grouping, the members of a single occupation or profession such as the army or the judiciary, or even a particular family.

When we write, as we have at the head of this chapter, *deux pays pour vivre*, we are, of course, making a plea for the autonomy of Quebec and Canada, acknowledging that both societies are nations in the full sense of the word, distinct from each other and from other societies in North America while still sharing a number of characteristics and experiences. But in recognizing the contradictions between us, respecting both the similarities and differences of the social projects we are engaged in, we will perhaps find a way to assure the full development of both. Of course, if you do not agree that

Canada and Quebec are unique cultures, then the task is very much easier; how to make the best deal we possibly can in selling out to the empire. The two Saskatchewan MLAs who formed a "Union" party in 1980 to promote the annexation of their region by the United States — because, as they said, "We have more in common with Americans to the south than with Eastern Canada" — were not unlike some Quebeckers who refuse to participate in the realization of a distinct society, saying that French Canada is too small and too weak to get along without being part of a richer and more populous Canada. Another variation on this theme of self-deprecation is English Canada's irritating habit of appropriating the "French fact" to define its own cultural identity. Though history can explain such attitudes, the plea we make here for our two countries is not to rectify or revenge the past. It is rather for us to take possession of the present and, armed with the means to determine a future for ourselves, to build a different place.

In his celebrated essay *Lament for a Nation*, which appeared in 1965, George Grant mourned the alleged disappearance of the Canadian nation. He wrote with passion of what had been and was no more, about what might have been but could never be. Curiously, and despite his subtitle *The Defeat of Canadian Nationalism*, the book was a springboard for an awakening of the Canadian political consciousness. It is still an influential and much-read basic text on Canadian nationalism. Obviously Grant's words struck a chord with his readers, but *Lament for a Nation* did not contribute to a dynamic political movement that might have inspired a generation of young Canadians, because Grant thought the future was dead.

The reason was simple. For Grant, nationalism meant Conservatism with a capital C — the federal Progressive Conservative party and John G. Diefenbaker, to be specific. The only alternative on his horizon was liberalism (with a small l), which, although more in tune with the present age of progress, was a philosophy that would inevitably preside over the dismantling of the Canadian nation. Grant's exposé of liberalism was brilliant and devastating, and in it he was the first to show the ideological dimensions of the process of colonization: "The power of the American government to control Canada does not lie primarily in its ability to exert direct pressure; the power lies in the fact that the dominant classes in Canada see themselves at one with the continent on all essential matters." If we had been serious about having a country after 1940, Grant says a little further on, we would have needed "some political creed that differed from the capitalist liberalism of the United States."

With hindsight, it seems a bit preposterous that Grant saw Diefenbaker's defeat as the defeat of an entire nation, although in terms of narrow partisan politics we have indeed had a Liberal government in Ottawa more or less ever since. However, the success of *Lament for a Nation* was in part inspired by a reaction against Grant's pessimism and lack of confidence in the people of Canada and Quebec. For while he clearly believed we could not expect our already compromised leaders to blaze the trail to independence and self-respecting nationhood, he assumed that a society's direction and vision of itself could only be generated within the ranks of the establishment. As the establishment in Canada has been assimilated, that transformation can never happen.

Our perspective is quite different. We believe that resistance to American hegemony has to be built on more than economic doctrines and political creeds. It has to begin by postulating a completely different type of society for Canada and Quebec.

In the following chapters, we will argue for a self-determining society or *société autogestionnaire*, in which a great many more of the important decisions would be made by people directly and locally, so that the burden of responsibility and expertise is dispersed more equitably and the role of the citizen correspondingly enhanced.

No doubt the constitutional experts, the men of money and power who claim that the world turns on money and munitions, will find we dwell too much on culture. But we believe that the most influential entities in the coming *fin de siècle* will be those globe-girdling industries of information, communications and culture—in short, the industries of the imagination and of individual and social consciousness.

One final consideration: in the last decades, we have become accustomed to thinking of world politics in terms of the bipolar competition between the US and the USSR. Anyone who criticizes one of the superpowers is seen to be siding with the other—the "If you're not with us, you're for them" mentality. Conflicts in various parts of the world, where one or both of the giants may be backstage, manipulating the situation, contribute to this bipolarism. Nevertheless, despite the increase in these tensions and in sharp contrast to the situation just a few years ago, many countries have given up the idea that a perfect society can be had merely by imitating the paradigm of one or another superpower. In other words, people have become critical of imperialism itself, whether it comes in a socialist or a capitalist package. We are beginning to realize that each society has to invent itself and decide for itself what type of set-up best suits its own circumstances. We do not automatically support state socialism just because we criticize American capitalism.

Our quest is to discover how our two countries can re-orient themselves in the declining years of the twentieth century. We firmly believe that the health of one depends upon the health of the other: that as Canadians become more conscious of the threat posed by the United States, they will better understand Quebec's desire for emancipation; that as Quebeckers gain an understanding of Canada and Canadian nationalism, they will become more sensitive to the effect of Americanization on their society. Out of this we believe Canada and Quebec can found a new association of lasting value.

Chapter 2

In the Shadow of
American Imperialism

The Story of Canada–US Relations

For Europeans, the American Declaration of Independence was an act of rebellion and political separation whereby the thirteen colonies seceded from the British empire. In North America, it signalled the end of a brief period of British rule that had lasted since the defeat of the forces of French imperialism in 1763. With the creation of the United States of America, a third claim was advanced for continental supremacy, and the ensuing war was thus as much a bid for American hegemony as a war of independence.

That claim, eventually extended to include the entire Western hemisphere, was enshrined in the Monroe Doctrine, promulgated by the fifth US president in 1823, which prohibited any kind of European interference in America's affairs. Europe should stay out and leave the Americas to the Americans. For all that, it was a time of increasing US interference in Latin America; and Monroe's announcement was itself preceded by two unsuccessful military attempts to bring what remained of British North America into the Union. From the conventional perspective, these were struggles between Washington and London, but both campaigns were nevertheless aimed directly at Canada. In the seven-year War of Independence it was tentatively established that Canada would not become a part of the new American federation. Thirty years later, the War of 1812 confirmed the verdict, only this time the Americans mounted an invasion to conquer Canada by force of arms. What had begun as a conflict over maritime rights, with the Americans challenging British control of the seas, quickly turned into a boundary dispute. From the Canadian point of view, the United States was exercising its continental ambitions. But if Canadians wanted to reject annexation (being offered in the guise of liberation from the British yoke), the odds against successful resistance were long: half a million inhabitants to 7.5 million Americans, and a garrison army of only five thousand to fend them off.

The Americans saw us as temptingly vulnerable. Henry Clay, in promoting the war, confidently assured Congress that "the militia of Kentucky are alone competent to place Montreal and Upper Canada at your feet." Thomas Jefferson agreed it was "a mere matter of marching." All the same, as it proved on the ground, 1812 was a Canadian victory. The Americans gained control of the Great Lakes, but British and native troops repulsed the invasions into Upper Canada and retained control of the Western fur country and the coast of Maine. Following the American burning of York on one foray, the Canadians carried out a retaliatory raid and burned the Capitol in Washington.

Canada's territorial losses in the war were actually sustained after hostilities ceased, thanks to the ineptitude of British negotiators who handed back to the Americans areas taken during the war, re-adopting the old 1783 boundaries. The western border was extended along the forty-ninth parallel to the Rockies, and Canadian access to the southern sections of the Western fur territory was blocked, precipitating the demise of the North-West Company.

The War of 1812 determined that there would be a separate political entity in the northern half of the continent, but it did not cure the Americans of their continental hankerings. Manifest Destiny was just emerging as a political ideology, and although it impelled American frontiersmen west, they did gaze northward from time to time. Threats of US invasion resurfaced during the Civil War and again in 1895 at the time of the Venezuelan crisis and the Spanish–American war. Confederation was in part a response to loud talk about annexation voiced by New England and Midwestern merchants. Obviously, Canada needed to consolidate and organize her own interests in contradistinction. And not a moment too soon, for the British empire was already in retreat; with the Treaty of Washington in 1871, British troops were withdrawn from North America, and Canada was left on her own.

The first phase of Canada's relationship with the United States was taken up with jockeying for territorial control through military (and occasionally diplomatic) means. By mid-century this had settled into economic competition. Trade between the two countries became the chief field of contact and conflict for the next hundred years; and, as we eventually came to realize, trade has been America's unique and supremely efficient way of going about setting up an empire. From the outset, Canada functioned as the northern hinterland to the United States, its economy based on the great staples of fur, fish and timber.

When Britain converted from mercantilism to free trade by repealing the Corn Laws in 1846, the entire economic rationale of the empire changed. Colonial governments were permitted to drop duties that discriminated against foreign goods and to set their own tariff rates. This paved the way for colonial self-government, but it also sent the colonies scurrying in search of secure markets elsewhere. Canada turned to the United States and negotiated a reciprocity treaty that removed tariffs on natural products entering the US, remaining in effect from 1854 to 1866. It also authorized reciprocal use of the Atlantic fisheries and the St. Lawrence–Great Lakes waterways. Canada marked the occasion by converting from sterling to a dollar currency.

The new turn in economic relations did not dispel old fears of US aggression; but these were now tempered by the profitable prospects of continentalism for some Canadian merchants. During the 1850s, the St. Lawrence canals and the Grand Trunk Railway projects were completed by Canadian businessmen who hoped to draw American trade north into Canada.

Although the United States was forced to accept our separate existence, it did not follow that Americans were convinced a nation should or could be fashioned out of the unification of the British colonies in 1867. The 1867 rebellions in Upper and Lower Canada were understood by them to be expressions of dissatisfaction with British rule and stirrings of republicanism. That some Upper Canadians (Goldwin Smith and others) proposed union with the United States in the 1880s was taken as further evidence that Canadians themselves doubted the plausibility of their national project.

Historian W.L. Morton, in his book *The Canadian Identity*, maintains that Americans have always fundamentally misunderstood Canada. In their eyes, the small pro-British élite that dominated Canadian politics for so long prevented British North America from finding its true destiny with the United States. Naturally enough, they set no great store by colonial loyalty, and as a result they discounted the strength and cohesion of the two nations that made up Confederation. The notion of autonomy evolving within a colony is simply un-American – nonsense in terms of their philosophy of liberty. For a long time, Americans refrained from direct intervention in Canada because they felt they could rely on the natural desire for liberty eventually to deliver our peoples into their Union.

Morton goes on to differentiate between the American and Canadian social contracts. Americans, he notes, are a people of covenant; their cohesion is based on a belief in the ideals expressed in their constitution. This trait manifests itself in three ways: in the tendency toward uniformity (the need to build a society with those of like mind); in the desire for isolation (the inclination to withdraw from or exclude non-participants in the covenant); and by imbuing national life with a strong sense of mission. The Canadian experiment is guided by an identical desire for a free society, but the basis of our contract is allegiance to the Crown – the personification of the law and the guarantor of Parliament. The progression of Canadian nationhood has therefore been demarcated by statute and treaty, precedent and tradition being the underlying principles.

In short, Morton says, the meaning of American society is the performance of a mission while the meaning of Canada's society (in contemporary terms, we would add Quebec's) is the working out of a destiny. However, because of their tradition of independence and revolutionary liberty, as embodied in republicanism, Americans have been prevented from seeing how the Canadian alternative could achieve freedom through evolution within the ancient institutions of Parliament and the monarchy.

With the introduction of the National Policy in 1879, Sir John A. Macdonald charted the course Canadian foreign policy would follow for the next century. It was essentially a balancing act between British and American spheres, using tariffs to navigate a safe passage between the Scylla of continentalism and the Charybdis of British imperialism.

"Equal existence" with America along with "free association" with the countries in the Commonwealth was the objective. Canada would be able to hazard collaboration with the US, provided it could preserve its options through other strong relationships.

Canada's nation-statehood was not achieved overnight. Diplomatic relations between Canada and the United States continued to be handled by London, until the humiliating finale of the Alaskan boundary dispute made it clear that the Canadian government had better look after its own foreign affairs. A department of external affairs was set up in 1909, although the US did not finally agree to accept a separate Canadian mission in Washington until 1920, by which time American investment in Canada was on the verge of outstripping Britain's. The attainment of full political autonomy under the Statute of Westminster in 1931 was to have no great impact on the relationship. The Americans knew they were in charge of North America by that time, and they pursued their interests with the same calculated and determined purpose as they demonstrated in the Alaskan dispute. From the turn of the century, US hegemony had been an "indisputable fact," and its global intentions were writ large. Teddy Roosevelt led his own private army up Kettle Hill in 1898 in defence of US business and in defiance of the US Constitution. As president he brought a tough, bullish and aggressive spirit — an aggrandizement of everything American — to government. He inaugurated the great age of US imperialism; Manifest Destiny was transported to a grander stage and the stakes upped accordingly. America would prosper and bring the blessing of liberty to the ignorant and beleaguered of the earth.

Despite their suspicions of US motives, neither the Canadians nor the British seemed very willing to oppose American pressure on Canada. Early on, the Americans discovered that in the event of conflicting interests, Canadian leaders could be counted on to compromise with a minimum show of strength. America got into the habit of taking Canadian goodwill and compliance for granted, so that by the time Laurier took to embellishing his high hopes for Canadian independence with statements like "The twentieth century belongs to Canada," Canadian economic integration with the United States was well underway. The irony is that as Canada gained freedom from Britain, new links with the United States were being forged that matured into even deeper liens on our sovereignty. As the country was drawn further into the US orbit, the relationship was dressed up in elegant official pronouncements; Franklin Roosevelt gave us his "good neighbour policy," and speechwriters began extolling the wonders of the "world's longest undefended border." Eventually, having emerged from World War II as the third-largest industrial-military power left standing in the West, Canada wanted to be promoted to junior partner in the imperial enterprise.

Throughout the history of Canada–US relations, these two factors have been at work. First, there is American disregard for Canadian nationhood (which the Canadian élite has internalized as part of its own philosophy). Again, according to Morton, America's ingrained misreading of Canadian society led the US to accept our nation without respecting or valuing it. Second, succeeding generations of Canadian policy-makers have taken to heart the idea that American superiority places immutable restrictions on our freedom to act. The question "What will the Americans do?" usually gets answered before anyone asks, "What do Canadians want?" Negotiations are conducted under a thinly veiled attitude of defeatism, the task for the Canadian side being to wrestle the "best possible deal under the circumstances."

Living next door to history's most powerful and technically sophisticated country, Canadians are as obsessed with America as Americans are blasé about Canada. For one thing, the relative size of the two populations leads Canadians to measure all manner of events and endeavours by that yardstick—the so-called ten per cent solution. Yet by world standards, our population and wealth are neither small nor insignificant. It is only our immediate proximity to the US that makes them seem so.

The elephant and mouse analogy may be a cliché, but it does convey some flavour of the experience. Whatever your opinion of elephants, the number one priority for all mice is to avoid getting stepped on, which means keeping tabs on those big feet at all times—becoming professional elephant-watchers. Mouseville is crawling with experts on any and all pachyderm activity. But if fascination with the US animates Canadian history, it comes in equal parts of admiration and loathing. As a people, we have not yet made up our minds about America; as a nation-state, we go on flattering ourselves that our association with the US is voluntary, when in reality it is dictated by the Americans.

For their part, Americans care little and have almost no

opinion or knowledge about Canada. Canadian affairs are strictly a matter for government experts and a few university professors running special Canadian studies programs at institutions such as Duke University. From the American point of view, Canada is so secure an ally that when conflicts do arise, they are referred to as mere "irritants."

But for all the problems that proximity to the United States brings, there have been positive aspects. If the Americans have taken Canadians for granted, Canadians themselves never have. The colonial version of our history in school curricula depicts this as a country created by default — the result of actions taken by other people in other places. The truth is that Canada, as much as any other country, is in a process of perpetual self-definition and re-creation. We have never assumed that the final form has been achieved. Perhaps this is why, when Confederation is actually one of the oldest living regimes in the world, we feel so young. To a great degree, Canada exists and has always existed because of a strong and determined desire to exist. This may be the most important truth we can learn from our past and bring to bear on the future.

Canada's experience with the United States is not unique; economic activity and trade has been the cutting edge of American imperialism wherever it has gone. US technology and enterprise, in their relentless pursuit of markets and materials, have carried a powerful and persuasive cultural influence to the four corners of the world, making the American way of life the world standard.

In the case of Canada and Quebec, the prime mechanism of US control has been the branch plant. Its origins go back as far as the 1840s, but it really becomes important to the Canadian economy with the introduction of Macdonald's National Policy. Construction of the railway had created a national transport system, linking the commercial and financial nexus of Montreal with the future bread-basket of the West, and at the same time mapping out a nation-wide market. With the erection of tariff barriers, the country could embark on a vigorous campaign to develop domestic manufacturing. The goal of the National Policy was to build a national economy based on natural resources, which would allow fledgling secondary industries to expand within a protected market, providing badly needed jobs. High unemployment was a cause for alarm at the time and politicians feared it would lead to a recurrence of massive emigrations to the United States.

Twelve years later, the success of the National Policy was put to the test in a general election; the Liberals attacked it head-on, advocating "unrestricted reciprocity" with the United States. Historian Donald Creighton called the 1891 election the most important in Canadian history. He saw the Conservative victory as a confirmation of the independent approach to Canadian industrialization, and as a rejection of direct linkages to the US economy.

The forces of reciprocity, however, did not lie down and die. Some Canadians continued to hanker after free trade. Western farmers, for example, flush with the wheat boom just after the turn of the century, were eager to gain free access to the American market. There was, in other words, some justification for the Liberals' belief that they were being handed a golden opportunity when the Americans offered to renegotiate reciprocity in 1911. What Laurier did not reckon with was the strength of the business constituency, which had by then come to depend on the National Policy.

Anti-reciprocity forces rallied around the slogan "No truck nor trade with Yankees." (They were actually perfectly willing to trade with Americans so long as the activity took place on Canadian soil, where profits could flow through a few home-made pockets.) They championed something they called "Canadianization," by which US firms would be induced to move some production across the border and set up as if they were Canadian operations. American branch plants were the offspring of the National Policy; according to some, its greatest triumph. By 1914, Americans had $881 million invested in Canada and 450 US companies had moved in to make themselves at home (heading the list: Coca-Cola).

But these were no ordinary visitors. Unlike British "portfolio" investment, which consisted of lending money for the price of the interest paid, American investment provided capital in exchange for equity, which is to say ownership, and partial or complete control of the enterprise. With portfolio investment, when the debt is repaid, the transaction is completed and the contact terminated; there is, to put it another way, a sunset on the indebtedness. With direct investment, however, the relationship is more or less permanent. In the first case, a debtor can regain his freedom by repaying the loan; in the second, there is no such option unless the investor is willing to sell and a separate agreement is concluded to that effect.

Between 1900 and 1914, US investment in Canada increased five-fold. By 1926 it had surpassed Britain's. By 1930, the loss of equity caused by American investment was making itself felt: Canada's mining and smelting was forty-seven per cent foreign-owned, the figure in manufacturing was thirty-seven per cent and increasing rapidly. The Depression did flatten the curve temporarily, but by then, the pattern and direction of American direct investment was already set. By 1950, US investment in Canada had reached $4 billion, and in the succeeding decade it underwent its greatest expansion. Whole industries came under American ownership, notably the petroleum and auto industries, the twin mainstays of the American economy. These achievements were consolidated in the Sixties and Seventies.

The United States and Canada have become each other's best and biggest trading partners, but the trade has never been equal, following the classic imperial pattern whereby the colony functions as a resource hinterland for the metropolis by exporting cheap raw materials and importing them again as expensive finished goods. Not much has changed since the days of the fur trade, and Harold Innis's famous staples theory, published in the Thirties, describes the present as aptly as it did the past.

It was Innis's argument that the staple-producing economy will never be transformed by industrialization but will remain a net exporter of resources and importer of manufactured goods, continuing to depend on borrowed capital and technology. He demonstrated in his exhaustive study of staple industries in Canadian history that the use made of resources, capital and labour has always been determined by absentee imperial powers—first France, then Britain and now the United States. It wasn't long before Innis's unconventional ideas were pushed aside (though his reputation as an important and original scholar survived) in the headlong rush of Canadian academics to embrace the tenets of American scholarship.

As levels of foreign investment soared, few Canadian economists raised so much as an eyebrow. Those who did break ranks with mainstream economic thought could quote Innis's prediction that as an economic satellite of the United States, Canada would never become a net producer of manufactured goods for the world market, because the profits generated in the industrial sector are not controlled here and are not allocated to building local industry. In the sanctum sanctorum of the Liberal party, Lester Pearson's finance minister, Walter Gordon, proposed limits be put on foreign investment and take-overs, but the measures he included in his 1963 budget were denounced far and wide in the business community and quickly withdrawn. Gordon himself followed soon after.

Then, as now, the Liberal party, Canada's traditional party of continental integration, was not easily diverted from its *métier* of steering foreign capital and American business into Canada. However, even during the heyday of the Sixties, cracks were appearing in the economy, revealing anomalies that were unexplained by orthodox economics. Gordon, Melville Watkins, Abraham Rotstein and others took a radically different approach. Picking up where Innis had left off, they instigated a revival of Canadian political economy by refusing to assume that foreign investment and ownership are neutral. They began by identifying the high level of foreign direct investment as an economic force in its own right; they studied the behaviour of foreign firms and their collective effect on the development of Canadian industry.

From the outset, the implied goal of US direct investment in Canada has been the capture of Canadian industry. Direct investment, by its nature, is related to and associated with ownership and control. It breeds institutional ties across borders that can be extremely difficult to dissolve. As the economy grows, the value and extent of equity investment grows with it; prosperity, which would normally enable a company to "pay off the mortgage" and take back control, produces just the opposite effect.

In a Science Council of Canada study of the multinational firm, economist Arthur Cordell points out that direct foreign investment is usually undertaken for three major purposes: to cultivate a foreign market intensively, when it is feasible and economic to do so by direct active control; to avoid tariff or non-tariff barriers or take advantage of lower costs, by setting up manufacturing abroad; and to develop or protect a source of raw materials.

Canada's chief importance to the United States has always been as a supplier of raw materials, and American investment has traditionally been most heavily concentrated in that area. As industry expanded in the United States, the pressure on domestic resource stores led manufacturers to seek replenishment from abroad in increasing quantities. Between 1939 and

1956, for example, imports of petroleum into the United States climbed from five to thirteen per cent of domestic consumption, iron ore from two to twenty per cent and lead from two to fifty-six per cent. From the American point of view, therefore, direct investment in Canadian resources was an efficient way of maximizing profit *and* minimizing the risks inherent in dependence on foreign sources of raw materials, satisfying all of Cordell's three purposes.

As we have said, tariff barriers can act as an incentive to foreign investment and ownership. In one or two special areas, the automobile industry being the prime example, the American-owned sector in Canada has grown big enough to lobby for and get complete elimination of tariff barriers. This was followed by a continental "rationalization" of the entire auto industry. Reviewing the behaviour of foreign corporate citizens in Canada, Kari Levitt in her book *Silent Surrender* attributes much of Canada's remarkable industrial expansion since the war to the internal growth of US affiliates. Aided by Canadian banks and financial institutions eager to lend them money to expand their branch plants, affiliates have been able to wax and prosper, importing less and less capital, all the while increasing their size and importance within the Canadian environment. The host becomes a servo-mechanism for the investor; the dependence, as Levitt remarks, is addictive, and the process, cumulative.

What would the balance sheet of US investment in Canada reveal, if such a tally could be drawn up? Levitt's research in 1970 showed that for $37 billion invested between 1900 and 1967, American business realized $130 billion, including retained earnings—an impressive 350 per cent return. In total, Canada sent $28 billion more in investment income to the US than it received during that period, and eighty-five per cent of it was generated within the latter two decades. However, the most striking change in the subsequent decade—the Seventies—shows up in the balance of payments column, particularly in current accounts. Here, accumulated debt has suddenly mushroomed, reaching a total of $75 billion by 1975 and averaging a $4.6-billion annual increase thereafter. Between 1975 and 1980 these increases added $23 billion to our international debt.

Meanwhile, industry by industry, the trade deficits have been mounting. Canada has the dubious distinction of being one of the world's largest per capita consumers of imported goods, and three-quarters of these imports are manufactured, compared with sixty per cent for the US and thirty-two per cent for the European Community. Against that kind of competition, manufacturing has always had a hard time surviving. The sector as a whole recorded a deficit in 1980 of $18 billion (up from the $3 billion reported in 1970), almost $2 billion of which occurred in the auto industry alone. (This industry, which had slight surpluses in 1970 and 1971, finished out the decade with a total deficit of $10 billion.)

Despite surpluses in the areas where we are strongest, such as agriculture and resources, the chronic shortfall in end products puts the balance of merchandise trade in the red year after year. To keep our current account afloat, governments have therefore fallen into the habit of borrowing more and more, to the delight of the New York money-lenders who have interest rates on their side. Since 1974, the annual value of new long-term bond issues has ranged between a high of $9 billion and a low of $2.5 billion; in addition, Canadian governments and corporations such as Hydro-Québec owe some $1 billion in short-term loans, a significant portion of them in the form of ninety-day notes. As some economists might admit, this puts Canada in a perpetual state of near-bankruptcy. Our balance sheet would also show that the outflow of dividend and interest payments (resulting from foreign borrowing and investment) has been rising to keep pace with the borrowing. The interest payments column has swollen from $900 million in 1975 to $3.9 billion in 1980. "The issue," as Arthur Donner writes in *Financing the Future*, "is that the current account is usually in deficit because of fairly substantial interest and dividend payments abroad, while on the capital accounts side, Canadian institutions rely quite heavily on US financial institutions and markets for their long-term financing requirements."

In short, economists are discovering not only that foreign direct investment is an enormous drain on the economy of this country and that it has grown by leaps and bounds over the years, but also that it has inhibited the development of Canadian enterprise by replacing it with American-controlled enterprise. Moreover, the change-over was actually financed by Canadian savings.

It leads one to wonder how much we have ever really needed foreign investment in the first place. If, by the end of the Sixties, as much as ninety per cent of American corporate investment in Canada was being raised in Canada through reinvested profits and borrowed funds, why could we not have simply financed the development ourselves, as we did with considerable success during the war, and retained ownership?

T.L. Powrie, an economist at the University of Alberta, provided a rather startling, if tentative, answer in 1977, in a study of the contribution of foreign capital to Canadian economic growth. He concluded that the net effect of foreign investment in Canada since 1950 had been to advance the national income only very slightly—by his calculations, only six months ahead of where it would have been anyway.

Still, even if it could be demonstrated that US investment vastly expanded the gross national product, we would not have proof that the standard of living was actually enhanced. For one cannot use the average national income, the GNP or any other single measure to gauge fairly the general health and well-being of a society. There are other considerations and many other "costs" involved that need to be evaluated in any cost–benefit accounting. Nationalist economists of recent years have recognized that American ownership of Canadian industry and ever-freer trade with the US are the pillars of a continental economy, and they have begun to look at the broader social and cultural side effects of the situation.

In many industries and corporations, the predominance of the American perspective has led to acceptance of the assumption that Canada is a northern extension of the domestic US market. Expedient though this may be for some Canadian businessmen, it does mean that Canada, like any other "region" in the United States, takes pot luck when it comes to production, even the production essential for a nation to maintain.

Lately, Canada has become a net importer of many basic items, such as food and furniture. But for federal tariffs and quotas, we would also have to depend on imported textiles and clothing. The capacity to produce life's essentials is, or ought to be, a matter of national security. Along with energy and defence, food and clothing must surely count as basic requirements for a country with a cold climate and a short growing season. Here too, the record of the multinationals in Canada has been negative.

The temptation to use Canada as a dumping ground for surplus production has been hard for Americans to resist, and dumping flourishes wherever opportunity and lax Canadian practice permit. As it happens, the cultural industries are among the most vulnerable to this sort of exploitation. For forty years, Canada was designated as a distribution outlet for

Hollywood movies. Arrangements among the major studios, distributors and theatre chains effectively controlled the North American market, so that a monopoly was allowed to exist that brooked absolutely no Canadian involvement in feature film production until 1968. Before the federal government set up the Canadian Film Development Corporation in that year, Canadians and Quebeckers had no choice but to live vicariously through the dreams and images of another society projected on the screens of their local Famous Players.

For American producers, Canada represents a safe, convenient ten per cent bonus market that requires little or no maintenance or cultural adaptation and can be satisfied with overruns from domestic production. Canadian producers, especially small and medium-sized firms, must compete against an astronomical cost advantage. For instance, a half-hour of television drama may cost $350,000 to produce but only $15,000 for a broadcaster to rent. All things being equal, the average Canadian manufacturer has a home-base market a fraction of the size he needs to recoup costs.

This is, of course, where tariffs and import quotas would normally be indicated, as the most common methods for a government to even up such odds. But it is now apparent that even those industries that have been singled out for protection have not escaped erosion. The Science Council maintains that Canadian manufacturing in general has been in decline for at least twenty years, and it points out that the condition is built into the structure and traditions of Canadian business.

The Auto Pact, for example, which some Canadians believed was intended to remedy our growing trade deficit by sharing production and protecting secondary industries such as auto parts, has proven to be no defence at all against powerful forces favouring US production — no guarantee against deficits and lay-offs. Orthodox economists, who base their theories on concepts of free trade and comparative advantage, are at great pains to explain why the pact does not benefit both sides equally; but then they do not allow for the role of the state in such matters.

The US government has a long-standing relationship with the US auto industry — as the saying goes, "What's good for General Motors is good for the country." Hard times in the form of cheaper Japanese cars, which brought one of the giants, the Chrysler Corporation, close to collapse, demonstrated indeed that what's bad for the American auto industry is also bad for America. A gentlemen's agreement to limit exports to the US was swiftly negotiated by the US and Japan. By tradition and by law, American government stands behind American businessmen: the Buy-America Act (in fact, a standard type of legislation with counterparts in many countries) requires that the government buy American-made goods when acquiring supplies, in effect reserving the purchasing power of the state for the support of domestic production. It is not only for security reasons that the Pentagon buys American when it buys armaments, it is sound industrial strategy as well.

Some Canadian economists have argued that the Buy-America Act contravenes the intent, if not the letter, of the Auto Pact. But we should understand here that from the American standpoint the Auto Pact was seen not as a protection for Canadian industry but as the prelude to full free trade in automobiles, which would restructure the North American auto industry into a single unit. The Canadian partners in the Auto Pact failed to appreciate the profoundly nationalistic character of American business and the thoroughly American brand of internationalism it practises.

Obviously, one result of foreign ownership in Canada is chronic unemployment. The natural tendency of the multinationals in organizing their operations has been to centralize, while taking as much advantage as possible of economies of scale. Labour costs, productivity, taxes and tariffs are taken into consideration when deciding where to locate production, but when all is said and done, a multinational is bound to be most sensitive to political pressure in its home country.

In manufacturing, especially, the tendency for branch plants is to reduce and simplify production by importing parts from elsewhere and assembling them locally. (Television sets sold in Canada are all now assembled from Japanese or American parts.) During recessions, pressure mounts to relieve unemployment at home, while host governments vie with grants and tax concessions to persuade Ford and the others to keep the branches open at all costs — to prevent the branch-plant economy from shrinking into a *warehouse* economy.

Various estimates have been made of the numbers of jobs lost to Canadians because of foreign ownership, but perhaps the most persuasive testimony is to be found in a US Tariff Commission report done for the US Senate Committee on Finance in 1973. The study, entitled *Implications of Multinational Firms for World Trade and Investment*, investigated the role of American transnationals in the US and in seven key foreign countries where US-based enterprises conduct the bulk of their activity: Canada, the United Kingdom, Belgium-Luxembourg, France, West Germany, Brazil and Mexico. Among the seven, Canada was distinguished for having absorbed the largest amounts of American investment, taking in $22 billion in 1970 compared with Europe's combined $24 billion and Latin America's $14 billion. We are also unusual for having "experienced the greatest MNC [multinational corporation] penetration of the industrial labour market," with US firms employing about one-third of the Canadian industrial labour force. (The next-highest was Belgium, with thirteen per cent.)

The study concluded that the impact of multinationals on employment, in all countries *except* Canada, has been moderate, which is to say commensurate with overall industry patterns. Only in Canada did their share of the total manufacturing employment *actually drop between 1966 and 1970* (though investment levels were still rising); only in Canada, Belgium and Mexico could the multinationals be said to be setting the trends, and only in Canada was their influence on employment clearly negative.

Another symptom of foreign ownership is what the Gray Report (Herb Gray's 1972 report to the federal Cabinet on foreign control and investment) termed truncation. Because of over-reliance on imports, especially parts and components for manufacturing, secondary and ancillary industry in this country languishes in a state of underdevelopment. In many cases, goods or services that could be produced here are supplied instead by parent or related companies located in the United States. At the same time, branch plants are routinely prevented from developing their own export capacity in order not to compete with a US-based relative, and this occurs no matter how much autonomy local management is reputed to enjoy.

It is often argued in defence of the performance of American subsidiaries that affiliates are incorporated Canadian companies and free agents, like any fully Canadian-owned firm. But whatever autonomy may exist can only exist if it is consonant with the strategic concerns of the parent company—that is, so long as the Canadian branch is compatible with and benefits its American parent. Autonomy is therefore conditional. Take Imperial Oil, a wholly-owned subsidiary of Exxon, which claims it is fully Canadian with its own board of Canadian directors. Nevertheless, in 1978, Imperial's president, Jack Armstrong, made it clear in testimony to the Bryce Commission on corporate concentration that he could not, in fact, adjust his budget more than $5 million on his own authority. At that time, $5 million would finance the sinking of two drill holes.

When we explore the limits of affiliate autonomy, it becomes clear that many factors of influence and control are far beyond the reach of local management — reliance on the parent company for technical expertise, for example. In the final analysis, one of the inescapable conditions of autonomy is Canadian identification with the parent firm and all it stands for.

Perhaps the most important index of Canada's industrial underdevelopment is the lack of research and development here. The international Organization for Economic Co-operation and Development (OECD) has research figures that show that Canada contributes as little as 0.9 per cent of its GNP to R & D, compared with Sweden's 1.6 per cent, France's 1.7 per cent, the United Kingdom's 2.1 per cent and the US's 2.4 per cent. This relatively low proportion of investment in research is a reflection of our dependence on borrowed technology, which is now becoming extremely expensive. It was in understanding the intimate tie-in of scientific and technical research with the development of a well-rounded industrial sector that the Science Council came to advocate an approach emphasizing R & D as the priority investment in future growth and self-sufficiency. The challenge has always been whether to put up stakes today that may pay off tomorrow. Only now are we realizing that there is a cost involved in consistently refusing to take the risk — an increasing dependence on imported technology and the loss of large chunks of our domestic economy.

As philosophers like Herbert Marcuse and George Grant have emphasized, technology is the handmaiden of empire. Marcuse writes in *One Dimensional Man*:

> Technology also provides the great rationalization of the unfreedom of man and demonstrates the "technical" impossibility of being autonomous, of determining one's own life. For this unfreedom appears neither as irrational or political, but rather as submission to the technical apparatus which enlarges the comfort of life and increases the productivity of labour. Technological rationality thus protects rather than cancels the legitimacy of domination.

Our dependence in this regard is perhaps the most telling indicator of our client status within the American empire. The massive importation of foreign technology creates a feeble ambiance in which to develop talent. Opportunities outside the branch-plant system dwindle, and the multinationals, who are also the largest consumers of high technology, typically reserve R & D along with policy control for head office. Their affiliates are rarely set up to do much in the way of original work.

According to the US Senate study, US-based multinationals not only dominate the development of new technology for American industry, but they are the principal institutions through which US technology in its various forms is exported or imported — and exports outweigh imports by a factor of ten to one (a net $2.3 billion in 1971, ninety per cent accruing to multinational corporations). Moreover, "as a matter of strategy, the MNCs do not, on balance, export their first-line technology either to their own affiliates or to unrelated foreigners. Rather, this first-line technology tends to be retained in plants at home, to generate new exports and compete effectively with imports in the same class."

The Canadian-owned sector of Canadian industry, in comparison even with the branch plants, has nickels and dimes to invest in technological development; in addition, Canadian business finds it much more difficult to raise venture capital from Canadian banks.

Entrepreneurial ability is usually thought to correlate with high incomes and higher education, which would seem to explain why technical expertise is most highly concentrated in affluent nations. How then can we explain Canada's lacklustre performance? Obviously, we have the education, the income and the inventive talent. Levitt postulates that branch-plant economies do not necessarily happen because native enterprise is lacking. In Canada, lack of enterprise is at least partly the result of branch-plant economies. Why is it that so many would-be local entrepreneurs and industrial scientists become salaried employees of the transnationals, eventually to disappear into the US? Because they are attracted to "the metropolitan, industrial and academic centre by high salaries, superior facilities and the fact that the professionals involved have internalized the values of the metropolitan society. By means of the 'brain-drain' the brightest and ablest people from low-income countries swell the technological resources of the richer countries."

Levitt's point is that while the negative effects of the multinationals can be blunted by government action of various kinds, the problems they bring to the host country are structural—that is, they are built-in. It is in the nature of American subsidiaries to thwart the development of a strong, independent and self-sufficient Canadian industry.

While it could be argued that the first loyalty of American transnational corporations is to themselves (or their stockholders), they also reflect American society and values. They are, after all, extremely important, highly visible and enormously powerful social institutions within the US. Their influence on American politics and business is not, as the Senate report would put it, negligible. That study, in fact, was primarily concerned about the impact of multinationals on American trade and employment. Specifically, the senators wanted to know whether there was any serious displacement of domestic production, caused either by importing from US affiliates abroad or by letting affiliates supply foreign markets. The answer, then, was no. Though a few industries indicated some loss of jobs, most did not and manufacturing gained considerably. So, too, the effects of the multinationals on US trade and its balance of payments was shown to be overwhelmingly favourable. However, ten years later, with unemployment in the US nudging double digits, there was evidence that when push comes to profits even American jobs could be sacrificed. No doubt the United Auto Workers, which agreed to wage cuts in 1982 in support of the ailing car companies, were aware of instances in other industries where production was moved "offshore" to take advantage of lower labour costs, particularly in populous and poor countries where the labour force is unorganized.

Nevertheless, such studies do testify to the enormous clout that multinationals wield. These companies are the centrepiece of American capitalism, the repository of its technological and industrial wealth, and the locus of its radiating military and economic influence.

Naturally, US domestic and foreign policy-makers recognize this fact and support US multinational corporate endeavour and prestige around the world. As Henry Fowler, the secretary of the US Treasury during the Johnson administration, once said:

Let no one forget the crucial importance to the multinational corporation of a United States government that commands world respect for its economic and military progress as well as for its commitment to the highest human ideals—a United States government whose political, diplomatic and military strength is fully commensurate with its role as leader of the free world—for let us understand that the United States Government has consistently sought to expand and extend the role of the multinational corporation as an essential instrument of strong healthy economic progress through the Free World.

Transnationals have a starring role in the American vision of world economic dominance and the pursuit of American goals and ideals.

Canada's new nationalist economists maintain that the price we are paying for US capital is US control and national disintegration spreading from the dry rot of our manufacturing sector. Foreign ownership unleashes forces that in the long run smother Canadian entrepreneurship and technological growth, and exclude Canadian investors from many important industrial fields. Canadian investment is confined to tertiary and service industries involved in the circulation of goods, rather than their production. The disproportionate flow of US capital into the primary resource sector creates severe capital scarcities elsewhere, particularly in manufacturing, which we have never been able to overcome. An unequal alliance has been struck between Canadian commercial or mercantile capital and American industrial capital, and rather than addressing the inequality, Canadian politicians have instead relied on mammoth transport and resource projects (pipelines and dams are favourites) that will give the balance of payments deficit a fix and postpone the reckoning—at least until after the next election. The only trouble is that once the effect wears off, the country finds itself still deeper in debt. As the dependencies and interdependencies proliferate, the autonomy not just of industry but of the Canadian nation-state itself is impaired.

If, as Mel Watkins argues in an unpublished paper, the role of the dependent state is to reproduce the conditions of its dependency—coping with foreign capital by alleviating the worst of its social excesses—then, strictly speaking, the state becomes an agent of foreign capital.

It is well known that the British Imperial State compelled the creation of the Canadian state, both by the Act of Union in 1840 and Confederation of 1867: the indigenous mercantile-financial bourgeoisie was left to work out, as it were, the details of the National Policy. The shift to American Empire exposed Canada to an imperial state whose impact in the Canadian context has been not with *state-building* but with *disintegration of the state*. (emphasis added)

With Mackenzie King at the helm, Canada entered the era of its greatest Americanization. Foreign investment was proclaimed the new wonder drug, enhancing the prosperity that close trade ties with the US would cement. In 1936, the prime minister signed a new trade agreement, in effect a reciprocity treaty, with the United States. Coming just four years after the Imperial Preference Treaty was concluded (the first such arrangement since 1846), it was naturally an inducement for American branch plants to use Canada as a beach-head for breaking into Commonwealth markets.

But it was C.D. Howe (an ex-American himself), acting as the chief executive officer of King's government, who moved Canada finally and firmly out of Britain's orbit and into Washington's. Under Howe's supervision, the branch plant was perfected as a system of continental integration; and with his blessing, the remarkable industrial base he built up in Canada during the war was turned over to American interests.

Much has been written and said of Howe's prowess as a businessman and industrial builder. As the compleat technocrat, the first of a breed that came to dominate Canadian business and bureaucracy with its ideals of efficiency and technical expedience, Howe was not a man of vision. The word was not even part of his vocabulary. His actions and policies were not informed by any particular concern or dream for the future of Canadian society. Much like the proverbial chicken's, Howe's purpose in crossing the road was usually to get to the other side. Since he was not given to sentiment or unnecessary high-mindedness, a larger meaning to his multifarious activities eludes us. In the end, his actions are their own telling legacy, and although Howe did not publicly espouse continentalism, he so identified with the culture and economic ideals of American business that he has come to represent that pole in Canadian history. Whatever he thought in his own mind, Howe was an effective ideologue, and his non-vision for Canada was, in reality, a defence of the American capitalist position.

Howe and his friends were helped by the fact that after the war, the West's economy did not sink into prolonged decline, as was expected, but took off in the opposite direction. There followed a period of unprecedented expansion that lasted into the mid-Seventies. While everyone was making money, it was too much to expect people to be critical about what was happening. Meanwhile, the Canadian state, in its various arenas of public policy-making, was rapidly aligning its outlook to match that of the United States. Defence policy soon followed trade into a continental system.

Having entered the war as an ally of Great Britain, Canada emerged as an ally of the United States. As a result of the defence alliance formulated by Roosevelt and Mackenzie King at Ogdensburg in 1940, a permanent Joint Board of Defence was set up and the Hyde Park Agreement of 1941 went on to provide the rationale for a continental war effort. Once the Americans became combatants, this board co-ordinated North American defence policy, involving co-operation on Canadian coastal territory.

After the war, it was a simple matter to establish the Joint Board as a permanent peacetime fixture. In 1947 King announced his decision to Parliament, and that year construction also began on the Pine Tree radar line (to be followed by two other joint warning systems, the Mid-Canada line and the DEW line), which was two-thirds financed by the US government.

At the outbreak of the Korean War, Canadian troops were first into battle alongside the Americans, solidifying Canada's close military allegiance. However, it was the Cold War that finally provided the Americans with the pretext for integrating North American defence. By the Fifties, weapons technology (atom bombs, jet aircraft and intercontinental ballistic missiles) had redrawn the world map of strategic conflict and Canada found herself lying in the path of a polar battlefield between Russia and the United States. For the first time, Canada became essential to the defence of the United States.

As the Russian threat loomed and the arms race accelerated, Washington (with Ottawa's approval) began planning a common air defence system for the continent that eventually became the North American Air Defence Command (NORAD), with its headquarters beneath a mountain in Colorado. The significance of NORAD's command structure (American commander and Canadian deputy) is more than symbolic, for it explicitly permits the commitment of Canadian forces to battle by US order. NORAD signalled the acceptance of American strategic doctrine as our own and allowed the infringement of Canadian sovereignty by the US through fear of the Cold War menace.

Though NORAD was the project of a Liberal government, it was given the go-ahead by Diefenbaker; surprisingly, the decision came within a few weeks of his first election victory of 1957. Some time later, General Charles Foulkes, who had been the chief of staff at the time, admitted to a Parliamentary committee that the Conservative government had been "stampeded" into the decision. Pushed or not, they certainly took their decision under circumstances of extraordinary informality, without the proper notification or involvement of the Department of External Affairs, without any written agreement, and without the consent of the House of Commons.

Judging from the debate that did ensue in the aftermath of the Avro Arrow débâcle, Parliament would probably have confirmed the move, which only underscores the fact that politicians on both sides of the House subscribed to the belief that Canadian and American interests coincided as a matter of course, as if by some law of nature.

Exactly that opinion was expressed at the time by Tom Kent (later to become Pearson's executive assistant and more recently chairman of the Royal Commission on Newspapers) in *Foreign Affairs*: "The first essential interest of Canada in the world today is the security of the United States; that takes overwhelming priority over everything else in Canada's external relations." The alternative of neutrality was never seriously considered.

In fact, it was left to commentators outside the political process to wonder whether Canadian independence was being compromised. One journalist, James Minifie, published an account of the progressive Americanization of Canadian defence policy in a slim volume entitled *Peacemaker or Powder-Monkey*. In making the case for neutrality, he criticized not only the government but also the opposition parties for their complicity in the submission to US policy.

Once Canada's defence establishment joined up with economic integration, could co-operation in defence production be far behind? Within two years of joining NORAD and following the cancellation of the CF-105 Avro Arrow, the advanced all-Canadian-designed supersonic fighter, a defence production sharing agreement was indeed concluded with the United States. After 1959, Canada never again embarked on a weapons development program of its own, buying most military equipment from American suppliers, starting with the already obsolete Voodoo fighter, which had originally been rejected by the RCAF in favour of the Arrow, and including the ill-fated Bomarc missile. The Canadian government tacitly agreed to abstain from such defence projects in exchange for a promised share of production *à la* branch plant, which is to say, production to American design.

Of course, the value of weapons development is not strictly limited to defence or national security. It is widely acknowledged that the arms industry (which now includes everything from space exploration to telecommunications to medical research) functions as the technological training ground for a nation's entire industrial base. Today it is commonplace, when billion-dollar weapons deals are at stake, for the purchasing country to demand not only jobs and production but a portion of the research — what are called technological transfers. So, as with the new F-18 fighter aircraft bought from McDonnell Douglas in 1980, those spin-offs were just as contentious bargaining chips as the F-18's $2.3-billion price tag, or, for that matter, its uncertain performance.

By the end of the Fifties, American interests had acquired an overwhelming influence in Canadian affairs, the relationship cemented, as we have seen, by agreements made outside the political process and without the consent (and often without the knowledge) of the Canadian people. Throughout this period, Parliament seemed to be blind, deaf and dumb to what was, in fact, taking place.

To this day, our politicians go on uncritically accepting US domination in Canadian affairs. Just how far we have come was revealed at the round of trade negotiations concluded in 1979 in Geneva between the ninety-eight member nations of GATT, the General Agreement on Tariffs and Trade. According to GATT's own definition, Canada's negotiators actually agreed to join the United States in free trade by 1987, by which time eighty per cent of the trade between our two countries will be duty-free — a far cry from the meagre fifteen per cent proposed by Laurier in 1911.

The implications for Canadian political sovereignty were there to be drawn by those intrepid enough to track the negotiations through their labyrinthian four-year progression. The event simply eluded the public, their representatives and most news reporters. Few journalists or editors bothered to ask where GATT had been leading us. Headlines like "Merger or Association with the US?" did not appear in the *Globe* or the *Financial Post*, presumably because neither publication cares to acknowledge the political implications. Still, Kevin Doyle, when he was business writer for the FP chain (he is now editor of *Maclean's*), was prepared to mention the unmentionable in an article for a small independent publication (now defunct) called *Report on Confederation*.

Doyle maintained that the *de facto* free trade between Canada and the United States will inevitably require political control of some kind.

> If, say, Washington wished to impose very high tariffs on Japanese cars, there would be nothing to prevent Japan from setting up a branch plant in Canada and exporting tax-free to the U.S. So a common level of external tariffs becomes a vital necessity and that in turn raises a vast range of foreign and domestic policies that have to be agreed upon and implemented.

Is this to be effected through agreed-upon rules of political association or through the exercise of US dominance?

Doyle goes on to cite a free-trade deal negotiated in complete secrecy between Canada and the United States in 1948, the details of which are still classified. (At the last minute Mackenzie King cancelled the plan, it is said, on the strength of one of his periodic tips from the beyond).We might surmise that the GATT procedure, being out in the open, is preferable, and the outcome less capricious. Possibly so, but it nevertheless is completely beyond all public accountability and control. Not even all of King's spooks could do much for Canada in this eleventh hour.

Looking back, we can see that the mild flirtation with free trade became hot and heavy in the Thirties. Slowly, inexorably, successive Canadian governments backed Canada into free trade, but since the rout of 1911, no political party has ever gone to the country to try to sell it. (None has gone out of its way to oppose it, either.) No doubt Laurier's trouncing was an object lesson for Liberal politicians, teaching them never again to try fighting an election over the issue of Canada–US trading relations. Instead, governments over the years have conducted Canada–US affairs without resort to messy and politically treacherous parliamentary debate, as if it were all a matter of routine administration. GATT negotiations were put in the charge of special diplomats, and their decisions were not submitted to the House of Commons for ratification as comprehensive policies or treaties. Only some enabling legislation is needed to fine-tune the regulations, and Canada will finally have reciprocity without so much as a polite cough to warn us of the fact. As a matter of national policy and a soon-to-be-accomplished fact, free trade lives in a political limbo — neither recognized nor discredited.

This is not to suggest, however, that the idea has no apologists or public advocates. Two prestigious research institutes, the government-appointed Economic Council of Canada and the privately financed C.D. Howe Institute, have been quietly promoting free trade in business and political circles for years. Both make the case that with nearly all industrial countries today producing for markets of 100 million or more, Canada cannot survive on its internal market alone but must seek association with the one large market at hand: the United States. The idea is also supported by some prominent Americans, who see in the energy crisis reason enough to start talking about a continental energy policy. Low-key and scarcely above a whisper intended for the ears of Canada's business élite, the pitch of the free-traders (or *freer*-traders, as they prefer) found sympathy among members of the Foreign Affairs Committee of the Canadian Senate, who have called for a free trade arrangement with the US.

If this represents the opinion of American monopoly capital, the Canadian-owned sector has developed effective vehicles of alternative opinion in the Science Council, the Canadian Federation of Independent Business and the Canadian Institute for Economic Policy. These groups reject continentalist industrial strategies and free trade as a solution to Canada's economic ills. Their position is summarized in the introduction to the Science Council's study of Canadian industrial underdevelopment, entitled *The Weakest Link*; it is worth quoting at length:

1. Canada and Canadians must accept that foreign direct investment in Canada is a powerful economic agent that modifies this country's present and future industrial and trade structure and performance. Furthermore, foreign direct investment in general has a negative effect on those aspects of the Canadian economy. Foreign direct investment is not a conspiracy. Simply (and obviously), the behaviour

of multinational companies does not support the long-term aspiration of Canadians for their economy and society. The solution must, therefore, contain initial *support for Canadian firms* as compensation for their more limited resources and must modify the economic environment in such a way that policies are designed to be consistent with a developing Canadian industrial sector.

2. Much attention has been given in recent years to theoretical gains from free trade with the U.S. But this would be a counterproductive step from the standpoint of Canadian economic welfare given the low level of Canadian competitiveness in secondary manufacturing and the dominance of U.S. subsidiaries in these industries. Much more well-directed effort is required to develop *Canadian* manufacturing strengths *before* gains can be made from future or current tariff remissions.

3. The only way Canadian firms can establish international industrial positions as successful end-product exporters, is to foster innovative product and process developments which can provide the basis of overseas marketing ventures . . . . This direction has been supported effectively by governments of other western countries: it is possible in Canada. The main problem is to convince government, business and labour, of the necessity for industrial change; the chief obstacles are lack of vision and leadership in government and labour, and the low level of entrepreneurial aggressiveness in the Canadian manufacturing sector.

Their argument, in short, is to support the Canadian-owned sector of industry and particularly to improve its technological capacity. The Science Council calls this a strategy of technological sovereignty. Today, we could say that a counter-ideology has grown up within the ranks of Canadian economists; and we can see that it has made some impression on public opinion—to the extent that P. E. Trudeau, the arch anti-nationalist himself, was moved to defend public involvement in the energy field through Petro-Canada and to promise a tightening-up of the Foreign Investment Review Agency during the February 1980 election campaign. The first bore fruit with the National Energy Program (which had the nationalists cheering and the Americans gnashing their teeth); the second promise was buried without ceremony under fire from free-enterprisers.

FIRA was set up in 1975 to review all proposed take-overs by foreign firms and to judge whether they would contribute "significant benefit" to Canada. So far, the agency has approved more than ninety per cent of the proposals brought before it, a record that prompted *Barron's* famous quip that the only American business that wouldn't be cordially welcomed to Canada is Murder Inc. On balance, as political scientist Wallace Clement puts it, FIRA acts more as a funnel than as a screen for foreign investment, its prime function being political, as "a great public relations exercise to 'cool out' nationalist sentiment" in the country. But it is reduction, not regulation, of foreign ownership that is required.

As understood by the stewards of the Canadian state, our destiny (and also Quebec's) is economic integration with the United States of America. Our industrial, economic, military and technological dependence has been fostered and perpetuated by government policy, in application if not by declaration.

Without ever seeking a mandate from the people, the Liberals, aided and abetted by the Conservatives and the NDP, have edged our country into a continental economy, claiming that events and conditions permit us no alternative. At the same time, we have also drifted into the American fold in defence and foreign affairs. In each of these areas, dependence on the US has meant the infringement of our national sovereignty, in the tangible sense that it has restricted our options and therefore our ability to act, to create and to govern our daily affairs according to our own ideals and priorities.

But the performance of American capital in Canada is not inconsistent with its effect elsewhere in the world, even if the relationship in our case is closer and more intimate than most. America acts as an imperialist power in Canada, an empire on its best good-neighbourly behaviour, but a subjugating force nevertheless. In Canada especially, modern American capitalism cloaks itself in the deception that human knowledge and technique are universal and apolitical.

Given the evolution of America's influence in cultural fields and the extraordinary power and reach of the new information technology, much more than economic or political autonomy is now at stake; we would do well to think about what happens to a society's consciousness, its collective imagination under these circumstances.

Culture in the Colonies

As George Grant observed, branch-plant economies do indeed breed branch-plant cultures. Our landscape is festooned with the evidence. As the technology of the mass media has advanced, so has the invasion of borrowed images, objects and words into our daily existence. Thirty years ago, the report of the Massey-Lévesque Commission on National Development in the Arts, Letters and Sciences expressed the commission's fears about the flood of American mass culture crossing the border. It referred to the need to meet these persuasive influences without the advantage of "what soldiers call defence in depth." But if the warning to secure Canada's cultural defences was heard, it was not heeded. It was not until the Seventies that the federal government was provoked by the gathering crisis in the cultural industries to consider the need for a cultural policy. Meanwhile, Warner Brothers, IBM, Time-Life and the other giant American corporations, who long ago assumed dominion over our cultural environment, continue their work virtually unchallenged.

Despite the blatancy of the American presence in Canada, nobody of any consequence at the top has seriously considered its impact on the evolution of Canadian society. As with the issue of foreign ownership, the authorities give some grudging recognition to the problem, but leave it to those affected to deal with it. Some of the cultural dimensions of continentalism were cursorily explored in the Gray Report and by Kari Levitt; yet through the Seventies, when the question of foreign ownership was brought up, even by nationalists, the cultural industries were still rarely mentioned. Partly this was due to a lack of basic information (Statistics Canada didn't start keeping track of culture until mid-decade), and partly, where English-speaking academics and critics were concerned, it was caused by lack of sensitivity to the issue. In both areas, the Eighties have brought some noticeable changes. Paul Audley was able to produce the first comprehensive study of the political economy of culture with *Canada's Cultural Industries* in 1983, and Stephen Clarkson's *Canada and the Reagan Challenge*, published in 1982, contains a major section on the environmental and cultural ramifications of our client-state status, detailing the difficulties we have dealing with problems like acid rain when neither the United States government nor American business in Canada sees it as a problem.

No matter what the industry, we are learning, the hazard

of too much foreign ownership is one and the same: the liquidation of local production and monopolization of local markets by foreign producers. With books or with motor cars, the continental way of doing things leads to the same result, the underdevelopment or complete disappearance of original Canadian production and, with it, the requirement that business pay particular attention to the social or cultural environment here.

As industries go, moreover, cultural industries—book and magazine publishing, recording, film-making and so forth—are both labour- *and* capital-intensive, and are highly dependent on original research and design. Each "product" has to be newly created from the ground up, incurring a whole range of start-up costs each time. There are some short-cuts, but every original book or movie implies a reinvention of the whole production process. It is crucial, therefore, that the industrial cycle of creation, production, distribution and consumption be complete and balanced so that the profits resulting from the whole operation are ploughed back into the development of new works.

In world terms, the size of the Canadian market for mass culture may be comparatively small, but we Canadians have a huge appetite for it—and the means to indulge ourselves. We are the world's most avid movie-goers and the largest foreign market for Hollywood films and American magazines and television programs. Our total expenditure on radio, television, recordings, books, magazines, newspapers and movies reached $5.6 billion in Canada in 1980, nine-tenths of it in the form of retail sales and advertising revenues, the last tenth being government expenditure. Yet most of this commercial activity bypasses the marginal Canadian-owned sector and ends up supporting more American production.

In the gross imbalance between domestic and imported, Canadian culture is the stranger playing a bit part on the Canadian stage. When Canadian and Québécois artists and producers set out with high hopes of capturing a native audience, they quickly find that space in the Canadian market has already been rented out on long-term lease to US industries, which have subsumed Canada and Quebec as an outlet for American products. Canadian work is effectively locked out. Various efforts to overcome this disadvantage have thus far only proven that, until the odds are evened and the ground rules changed, Canadian culture will continue to exist as a subculture—and then only so long as it receives massive government subsidy.

Foreign ownership in the cultural industries has meant the under-utilization of Canadian talent and facilities. (A major study of the film industry by the secretary of state's department in 1976 estimated that it was then operating at fifty per cent capacity.) It has also created structurally induced incentives for Canadian producers to imitate the foreign product, in the hopes of riding to fame and fortune by means of well-merchandized American formulae. Even broadcasting, the one cultural industry publicly regulated and Canadian-owned by law, experiences overwhelming competition from one source—the United States. From our history, we know that, left to its own devices, US capitalism will move in and install a monopoly to guarantee its access to the Canadian market, blacking out Canadian production. What we have inherited, then, is virtually a 100 per cent quota for American culture, which no amount of ministerial hand-wringing or voluntary compliance has been able to dislodge.

Federal government investment in Canadian feature films succeeded for a brief time in the early Seventies when a host of talented young directors (Gilles Carle, Claude Jutra, Don Shebib and Allan King) were able to bring their creations to the screen. A national cinema could be seen taking shape in Quebec and Canada. Then, suddenly, a new type of hustler-producer pulled into town, dollar signs in his eyes and plane tickets to Hollywood in his back pocket. Production boomed; 100 features were made and $300 million invested in the last three years of the decade. What made it all possible was the introduction in 1976 of a 100 per cent capital cost allowance, which allowed full write-offs for private investors in films—a deduction previously provided in only two other fields, oil exploration and housing.

Back in the Fifties, enterprising Hollywood producers had invented the "quota quickie"—an American film produced in Canada for the purpose of end-running Commonwealth trade barriers. The Seventies version of this give-away provided Canadian producers with a honey-pot for attracting American capital and talent to Canada, while dealing themselves and a few local financiers into the profits. The results were such all-Canadian features as *Meatballs* and *Porky's*, and the Canadian film industry won the title "Hollywood North."

In a classic case of bad money driving out good, the start made by Canadian directors and film-makers in developing a genuine national cinema was abruptly ended. Film-making in Canada was converted (one is tempted to say "perverted") into deal-making. Tax accountants, lawyers and producers took over, raking off fees in the order of $250,000 to produce phoney Canadian films. Hollywood-based Canadian actors found they could make twice their usual fees working in these pictures, because their names had acquired double the normal value as points for Canadian certification by the Department of Communications. But most of the producers who climbed on the bandwagon were more comfortable with American stars, script-writers and directors anyway. Believing that the only way to break into the big time is to follow the American pattern, they spent their creative energy ferreting out loopholes in the regulations. Gone was any pretence that the object of the exercise was cultural; while stockbrokers packaged the deals, artistic concerns were shunted off to oblivion.

The capital cost allowance caused a boom in Canadian film-making during these years, but it was a boom that bypassed many of our very best actors and directors. It was also quickly exhausted. Predictably, the movies it did produce were disasters, and a significant number never even received commercial distribution. The Canadian public, who patiently underwrote the experiment to the tune of hundreds of millions of uncollected tax dollars, got precious little in return. But by 1980 the abuse was so outrageous and the results so laughable that all three parties running in the federal election promised to tighten up the regulations.

Still convinced that a way can be found to make silk purses from sow's ears, the government decided, after a decade of pressure from the cable industry, to license pay-TV. In February 1983, two national and four regional services started up, their schedules packed with American movies and other imported fare. While the CRTC declared at the outset that pay-TV's only reason for being would be to infuse new funds into the ailing Canadian production industry and to provide more airtime for Canadian programs, the usual combination of economic imperative and the profit motive have, so far, produced the predictable results—little original Canadian production, but a chance to make our own soft-core porn for pay-TV's late-night Playboy audience.

Early in this century, when film-making was in its infancy, many governments, including Canada's, got into film-making and broadcasting because they could see that state involvement was the only way to preserve the public interest in these fields.

It was already evident that the new media possessed magic powers of persuasion and enchantment. Since the Thirties, Canada has maintained a public presence in both film and broadcasting through the National Film Board and the CBC—but not without a certain ambivalence. Over the years, Canadians have been deeply influenced by the American belief that mass media—the main systems of cultural communication —should be left to the private sector to develop. Despite the fact that the United States is the outstanding exception to common practice throughout the world in this respect, Canadians have accepted wide-open commercialization as the norm, an approach consonant with the "immutable laws of business."

As it has in other fields of endeavour, proximity to the US has distorted our view of public enterprise, which some Canadians perceive as emasculated or failed private enterprise. But to see our economic landscape as some kind of substandard version of the American scene is to misunderstand profoundly the nature of Canadian economic culture. As Herschel Hardin sets out in his book *A Nation Unaware*, a good many public enterprises, particularly those inherited from private interests gone bankrupt, are reactions to American initiatives; but they are also projects that a small, sparsely populated nation could support no other way. Of course, the perversity of Canadians in denigrating rather than valuing this experience is an intriguing aspect of the Canadian identity.

> The economic dimension of Canadian identity is weak.... At the centre of this fragility ... is our inability to accept one of the most vibrant expressions of the Canadian character—Canadian public enterprise. It is usually taken for granted that Canada is a free enterprise country, after the United States and its Americanism, and that the native public enterprise tradition is therefore a somehow secondary or untrustworthy, even marginal phenomenon, although it exists on a substantial scale and in most sectors of the economy. But citizens of an ideological colony cannot take anything for granted. They have got to make their own analysis. And when they do, they are liable to discover an unexpected originality in themselves.
>
> In Canada's case, the explorer of the colonial ideology begins to feel like Alice in Wonderland. The more he pursues his investigation of the

Canadian experience *in its own terms* — in this case, in terms of the contradictions between itself and the United States — the more it appears that Canada, in fact, is a *public* enterprise country, and that native *private* enterprise is a somehow secondary, untrustworthy phenomenon, although it exists on a substantial scale and in most sectors of the economy. So that the received colonial image of Canada as a free enterprise country must therefore be upside down. The American-ideology-in-Canada, with all of its phantasmagoric potency, stands Canadian reality on its head.

Hardin explains further that the uniform individualism that characterizes American society makes it a private-enterprise nation although the nation itself is not an enterprise. With Canada, the opposite is true. Economic organization has often been the product of nationalism rather than the producer of nationalism as in the American case. The big economic questions in Canadian life have had nothing to do with celebrating or defending economic individualism, but with "bringing the parts into the whole." Canada is itself a public enterprise.

For a host of reasons, the mass media in this country have been developed (good intentions in broadcasting notwithstanding) mainly by private, commercial interests. Consequently, they have been turned into vehicles for distributing American culture and promoting the American way of life. For the process of Americanization does not come only by way of branch-plant operations or heavy reliance on imports, it is embedded in the commercial process itself.

Anthropologists and historians, looking back on our civilization, may well see the capitulation to American mass media as the Waterloo of Canadian independence, after which all resistance to assimilation evaporated. Certainly the cultural industries, where the importance of original Canadian production should have been self-evident, have never been protected, but have been allowed instead to struggle under American domination.

If economic efficiency were all that mattered, most of the world's publishing could be turned over to two or three giants, just as petroleum refining is. However, a country that cannot publish its own books will not develop a national literature of indigenous character. A national literature is not something you can purchase wholesale. Nor can its existence be arranged by adopting commercial practices and standards of excellence imported from some other country, no matter how excellent that country may be. A 1966 UNESCO study of the world book trade expressed the dilemma this way:

> If [these countries] are to receive books "bestowed" from outside ... without the contribution of minority languages (and culture) then the emerging reading public will be doomed to passivity and excluded from that active participation which distinguishes real literary life. *A mediocre literature in touch with its own people is better than a good literature which is deaf to the voices of those to whom it is addressed and whose feelings and thoughts it should express.* (emphasis added)

If mass culture has been largely abandoned to the vagaries of American commerce, élite culture in Canada has been organized on the basis of public subsidy, that is, public enterprise. Nevertheless, a pattern of private control and imported culture is evident here, too.

The institutions of official culture (the Canadian Opera Company, the National Ballet, the Stratford Festival) are, by and large, incorporated as non-profit, but still private, corporations. A few were set up as statutory institutions (the National Arts Centre and provincial museums, for example), but as a group, they all rely on the same mix of public and private funding in the form of tax-deductible "charitable" donations. Harking back to aristocratic origins in Europe, when the Louvre was the personal art collection of the king of France, this financial encouragement to the producers of élite culture is still called patronage. Indeed, contemporary government patronage of the arts does constitute a form of political patronage in the modern sense as well, in that it involves granting privileges to some groups and individuals and not to others.

Today patrons sit on the boards of cultural organizations — not as the volunteer helpers they are often made out to be, but as directors, making policy, deciding on artistic direction and hiring and firing administrators. Political scientists John Porter and Wallace Clement, who have studied social class in Canada, have shown how political and economic élites form relationships, make deals and maintain their contacts and positions of control through old-boy networks, at private parties and restricted clubs, and on boards of prestigious art organizations. The introduction of public subsidy—one of the results of the Massey-Lévesque Commission—did not mean that membership on these boards would be opened up to the public; even the appointments made by governments are usually made on the advice of the existing board, to avoid offending tradition.

But public subsidy did bring some changes. It created a climate for artists to be treated more professionally—that is, to be paid for their work—and it provided the means to build better facilities and organize tours to outlying areas. Still, despite recognition that the arts are the heritage of all citizens and, like education, cannot be self-supporting, arts boards do not yet represent the communities they serve.

Moreover, we can say without fear of contradiction that the programs of any theatre company or art gallery will tend to reflect the preoccupations and biases of the group that dominates its board. For their part, governments and arts councils that distribute the public's largess to the arts do so according to the principle of arm's-length involvement, whereby the receiving institutions are free to support whatever art they deem important or excellent.

Given the predilection of the Canadian élite for measuring itself in terms of the US, taking its cultural cues from the same people it looks to for business leadership and loans, this group has, on balance, done very little to understand, encourage or promote Canadian art. Its main achievement has been to build institutions capable of producing first-class theatre or ballet or opera in Canada. By and large, this patron class does not see its responsibility as helping to build Canadian theatre: plays written, directed and acted by Canadians for Canadian audiences. In Canada and Quebec, the upper classes have fastened their ambitions on "world-class" art, which is essentially European in derivation but international only in the sense that it has long since lost affinity for any particular national culture and is today practised by a consortium of countries.

These days élite culture as such is neither American nor even capitalist. The superpowers are also supercultures, with world-wide mass media networks distributing centrally planned, conformist cultures. In this sense, the United States has indeed become the greatest show on earth. But as we have suggested, we find the culture of the international set— paralleling mass culture and in a kind of stratosphere of its own—put on display in the art palaces of the world's capitals:

Covent Garden, La Scala, Lincoln Center and Moscow's Palace of Congress. The Soviet Union and the United States vie for pre-eminence in space, in sport and, yes, in ballet. What better propaganda coup than the defection of a ballet dancer?

Just like American mass culture, the institutions of official culture in Canada and Quebec offer programs of remarkable similarity to each other that contrast sharply with the actual regional and cultural diversity of contemporary Canadian society. The near-exclusion of local art, both contemporary and historical, is justified according to the ideology of excellence. A commitment to the pursuit of what is, in the end, a matter of judgment and opinion, *not* of fact, enables arts institutions to absolve themselves of responsibility to anything "less than excellent." And if — by the definitions and standards of greater, more "civilized" societies than ours — excellence cannot be found in Canada, then it is easy enough to import.

In short, geography and the outlook of continentalism have positioned our mass and élite cultures within easy reach of American enterprise, which hasn't failed to exploit the situation. This has achieved two things for us: it has fostered a cultural establishment prejudiced against Canadian culture, with an economy structurally inimical to it; and it has erected an invisible pipeline, one that flows only one way, as the oil and gas lines do, but in our direction, disgorging a torrent of American information and images into our cultural environment.

Although the French language has slowed Americanization in Quebec by making local production an absolute necessity, the barrier has not been impenetrable. Quebec society has also fallen under the spell of American-style technology and consumerism. Industrialization and urbanization happened relatively late, but Quebec now subscribes to the American way of life with as much enthusiasm as does the rest of Canada. In the Sixties, Quebec writers, film-makers and publishers found, as their Canadian counterparts were soon to discover for themselves, that trying to speak directly to a local audience was inevitably to challenge imperial taste and, eventually, imperialist economics.

The Quiet Revolution and After

Nineteen sixty: the year Maurice Duplessis's Union Nationale was finally defeated; the beginning of the Quiet Revolution. The Quebec question has dominated the political agenda of this country ever since, with only the odd intermission. But along with a change of government, Jean Lesage's Liberals ushered in an ambitious programme of reform that launched what amounted to a thorough overhaul of Quebec society. A generation of well-educated Quebeckers, the new French-speaking middle class, guided this transformation from positions in the rapidly expanding provincial civil service and in public institutions such as the recently created secular school system. At the time, jobs in the public and para-public spheres were all that were available to francophones, opportunities in the exclusive, English-speaking world of business being notoriously scarce. But in the latter half of the Seventies, this picture started to change. For many reasons, including the positive results of the PQ's Bill 101 (effective even in the C.D. Howe Institute's estimation), a French business milieu was developing and Quebec enterprise flourished along with it.

The Quiet Revolution has already been written into history as the great watershed that changed Quebec irrevocably. But long before Liberals like René Lévesque and Jacques Parizeau took up the call of sovereignty–association, rank-and-file Quebeckers were taking increasingly radical political positions in their unions, in the student and women's movements, in their community associations and in their poetry and song. People began talking of independence; Quebec very clearly was on the move. Bombs appeared in Westmount mailboxes; there were mass demonstrations; English bosses were burned in effigy, and English Canada soon got the message. Finally, after a series of especially tough articles by André Laurendeau, editor of the Montreal daily *Le Devoir*, the Pearson government was sufficiently alarmed to set up a Royal Commission on Bilingualism and Biculturalism, making Laurendeau co-chairman with Davidson Dunton and promising language reform. That was 1963.

In English Canada, the Quiet Revolution has generally been understood not as a social or cultural phenomenon but as a series of date-lined political events. It has been described in the gross journalistic terms of news reporting. The referendum campaign of 1979–1980 was a case in point. The details were covered, but little of the atmosphere of the place or the flavour of the arguments—the scare-tactics as well as the intellectual bickering—was conveyed. Obviously more is at issue here than the fact that the seamy side of the story wasn't reported outside Quebec; it is that so little thought and reflection is given to Quebec by English Canadians beyond its significance as a political and constitutional riddle. In most of

English Canada the Quebec question boils down to bilingualism, which is to say *flocons de maïs* on cornflakes boxes. The efforts by a few Canadians to respond by proposing a project for the renewal of the English-Canadian side of the "two nations" equation received more attention in Quebec than in English Canada, where political leaders are still reacting to Quebec rather than taking any positive initiative.

Of course, the political history of Quebec through the Sixties and Seventies does make a terrific story. The raw statistics alone are extraordinary: five premiers, four governments formed by three different parties, including one that has since died out (the Union Nationale) and another that was barely a decade old when swept to power. The changes also brought a more progressive national spirit to provincial politics; for the Quebec electorate, infected with the taste for reform, had rising expectations of its representatives. The evolution can be traced through the political slogans that came and went with the elections: *C'est le temps que ça change*, 1960 ("High time for a change"); *Maîtres chez nous*, 1962 ("Masters in our own house"); *Égalité ou indépendance*, 1967 ("Equality or independence"): *Égal à égal*, 1979 ("Equal to equal"). By the end of the Sixties, it was no longer possible for anyone contemplating a political career to ignore Quebec nationalism. As recently as 1981, when the Liberals under Claude Ryan failed to oust the PQ, there was bitter criticism within party ranks that the Liberals had self-destructed by failing to speak to that very sentiment.

Without doubt, one of the noisiest battlefields during the Quiet Revolution was the arena of federal–provincial relations. Quebec and Ottawa bureaucrats clashed with each other on a regular basis over fiscal policy, immigration and social welfare programs, with Quebec charging that the federal government was attempting to spend its way into fields not under its jurisdiction, and challenging it every step of the way.

Plagued by Quebec's escalating demands, Prime Minister Trudeau convened a series of first ministers' conferences to come up with constitutional reforms that he hoped would satisfy the Quebec government's need for special status without fundamentally altering Confederation. The impossible task Trudeau set himself was to head off the separatist movement without conceding Quebec's existence as a nation, even within Canada.

His immediate answer was the federal policy of bilingualism —a curious breed of bilingualism, though, in which only government bureaus and services, but not individuals, were required to operate in both languages. This was soon joined by an official policy of multiculturalism, which meant Quebec could be disguised as an ethnic culture "like any other" and its distinctiveness could thus be acknowledged on grounds of free cultural choice, thoroughly palatable to liberals.

Meanwhile, the Quebec state (as the provincial government took to calling itself) assumed the role of chief participant and agent in social and economic development. As Quebec modernized, its birth rate fell from the highest to the lowest in Canada, putting the government in the position of finding some means of stemming the erosion of the French language. According to demographers, the language was in decline; in communities outside Quebec it was rapidly disappearing, and the long-term prognosis for its survival, especially given the developing mode of high-speed communications technology, looked grim even in Quebec. The obvious place to turn to for action was the National Assembly, which Quebeckers had already come to rely on more than the House of Commons, where their particular concerns have always had to be met through an anglophone majority.

As the most lively arena of Quebec's political culture, the electoral scene became a high-profile forum for philosophic and ideological exchange. The debate originally began in the Fifties, among a small group of intellectuals, journalists and unionists who loudly denounced the cosy, self-serving alliance between church and state. In the Sixties, it spread among the youth and workers to become a much more diversified and far-reaching protest. The initial period of dissent was followed by one of intense political activity in which everything about Quebec society was held up for re-evaluation. The dissenters, many of them veterans of the 1949 Asbestos strike (Trudeau and Gérard Pelletier included), had coalesced around the magazine *Cité libre* to champion the ideals of modernization and wider political participation—*Démocratie d'abord*, the masthead declared.

It has been said of *Cité libre* that its crowning achievement was Lesage's election in 1960, made possible because of the ideological groundwork laid by the magazine over a decade. Certainly the reforms that followed were very much in the *Cité libre* spirit. Denis Monière, in his book *Le Développement des idéologies au Québec (Ideologies in Quebec: The Historical Development)*, describes the Quiet Revolution as a cleaning-up and clearing-out process that had, in fact, very little revolutionary content. It only seemed so because of the rapid rhythm of transformation that it set in motion after a long period of stagnation. The Lesage government's programs were far more imitative than innovative; nationalization of hydro, reform of the civil service and secularization of education simply meant catching up with the rest of the industrialized world.

Naturally, along with this came a much enlarged public service and huge increases in provincial expenditures; the annual increase for the five years following 1960 doubled the average of the previous five.

As so often happens in human affairs, once the orthodoxy of the Duplessis era was broken, the ideological floodgates swung open, leading to what was perhaps the single most important accomplishment of the Quiet Revolution: Quebec's discovery of its own imaginative voice, its *prise de parole*. As Monière writes, the Quiet Revolution was a mental unblocking. Projects for a modern Quebec society were no longer limited to musings of an editorial board but came to be recognized as necessary and valuable by everybody. "Respect for tradition," the byword of the previous age, was succeeded by phrases lauding the "challenge of progress," accompanied by an ebullience and self-confidence about assuming responsibility in economic and political affairs.

After 1960, nationalism, which had for decades been the preserve of reactionary conservatism, found expression in a variety of political theories — from liberal to social democratic to socialist, and all the way to the extreme of the Front de Libération du Québec. For the first time, a left nationalist analysis was advanced, and once again it was centred around a magazine. *Parti pris*, as its name proclaimed, took a committed position, locating itself in the middle of those forces pushing for the decolonization and complete restructuring of Quebec society. Its position was influenced and inspired by anti-colonial movements elsewhere, especially the Algerian revolution, and the writings of Frantz Fanon (*The Wretched of the Earth*), Albert Memmi (*The Colonizer and the Colonized*) and Jacques Berque (*The Dispossession of the World*). *Parti pris* advocated political action and for a decade watched over the arrival of new parties and movements, most of which disappeared or merged into other configurations: the provincial NDP, the Parti socialiste du Québec, the Rassemblement pour l'indépendance nationale, the Rassemblement national and the Mouvement pour la souveraineté-association. All of them, in one way or another, were precursors of the Parti Québécois. Citizens, community groups and committees of all kinds were affected by the climate of political assertion. Quebec broke out in a rash of political action groups (known as the CAPs: *comités d'action politique*), which took up the causes of women, the poor, living and working conditions, industrial safety and so forth but led inexorably to the one over-riding issue — the question of Quebec independence.

However, *Parti pris* was more than a crucible of ideas, it was a social catalyst, and a cultural phenomenon itself. Shortly after the magazine appeared, a publishing arm was established, also called parti pris, which over the years published some of Quebec's most important writers — Paul Chamberland, Pierre Vadeboncoeur, André Major, Pierre Vallières and Gérald Godin, among others. Moreover, parti pris poets and novelists belonged to that circle of artists, singers and film-makers who were to become symbols of Quebec's *épanouissement*, its surge of creative energy and its maturation as a society. They were made the spokesmen for political change and became tremendously popular in the process. The songs of Gilles Vigneault, still sung today by everybody, at any and all occasions, have been unofficially adopted as a kind of national anthem; when René Lévesque returned home after losing, ten to one, in the constitutional accord of November 1981, his Cabinet ministers came to meet him with a rousing rendition of "Gens du pays."

As Quebec struggled to remake itself in the midst of political upheaval, it seemed the population was in full flight from the patterns and traditions of the past. But in reality, Quebeckers were engaged in what the sociologist Fernand Dumont called an extraordinary pilgrimage back to their origins. Dumont describes the paradox in *The Vigil of Quebec*.

> In popular song, in poetry, in historiography, and in many other areas, the Québécois are penetrating to the depths of their collective existence, and although they have never before demanded such an accounting of their traditional institutions, they have also never gone farther in expressing their need to regain values inherent in the story of their own people.

Of course, the return to tradition, albeit reinterpreted tradition, was as good for morale as it was for art. It provided a reassuring context for all the change; the whirlwind, it turned out, had origins and could be given direction. Nor did the role of the "artistic" element escape the attention of the authorities, who, at the time of the crackdown in October 1970, gave Quebec's artists and entertainers top priority on their arrest lists. That dreadful ordeal was later recounted by Michel Brault in his powerful film *Les Ordres*, which was televised by Radio-Canada to the four corners of Quebec not long before the 1976 election.

The CBC's role in Quebec's emancipation is one of those lovely Canadian paradoxes—it is a federal institution that helped Quebe find its voice. In the Fifties, public radio was instrumental in breaking down the isolation of Quebec society, widening people's horizons and putting them in touch with others beyond the narrow confines of their parishes. Radio-Canada helped Quebeckers to think of themselves as a larger, national entity. It has also had an enormous influence on the French spoken in Quebec. Circumstances dictated that radio and television programming had to be produced locally, which meant that Quebec producers had no choice but to create for a local audience. This meant that French became a rich creative medium in its own right and achieved a hitherto unparalleled importance as a public langauge and conveyor of information and ideas. In this sense Radio-Canada lived up to the spirit and the letter of the Broadcasting Act and its social and cultural responsibility as a public institution. By contrast, English Canadians have not been nearly so well served by the CBC.

As we have said, in sociological terms the Quiet Revolution signalled the arrival and rise to power of a French-speaking middle class. It also altered for all time the balance of power between the francophone majority and the anglophone minority in Quebec, breaking the mould in which the two ethnic groups had been cast by history. The segregation by caste of the two societies, the English bankers and engineers and the French farmers and priests, was ended. But despite the great improvements of the Sixties, despite having turned themselves squarely to face the future, Quebeckers have still not decided what kind of Quebec they want to build—what type of society they want to become. The Quiet Revolution is not yet over.

Perhaps lack of clarity on this essential topic compounded the confusion about sovereignty–association that permeated the referendum campaign of the Parti Québécois. A decision on a new political structure was being called for, but before its guiding principles or *raison d'être* had been established. The debate about the future Quebec, begun in the Sixties, was put on hold while the Parti Québécois took sovereignty–association to the electorate. Fundamental questions about the distribution of wealth and power, the equality of women, the conditions of the poor, conservation and energy, and the rights of all citizens to participate in planning and decision-making were set aside.

The Quiet Revolution had offered up several possibilities about the direction Quebec might take. *Parti pris*, among others, argued for independence and socialism; the Liberals argued for federalism, "French power" and American technocratic capitalism. But as the debate focussed more and more on the National Assembly, it narrowed. After the PQ came to power, social research once done by many people, including the *citélibristes* and *partipristes*, was largely taken over by Camille Laurin's superministry of cultural development. The discussion was parcelled out in White Papers, almost as if the whole thing had been nationalized.

And yet during these years—the Seventies—the most striking change in the new Quebec was the increasing Americanization of the urban middle class and the mass media. Here, where we would have least reason to expect a party of national independence to falter, the Parti Québécois declared no contest. That issue, too, was shelved until after sovereignty was settled; and there it remains.

English Canada's Silent Revolution

If the Quiet Revolution has in any way been overrated, then the changes that took place in English Canada in the same period have definitely been underrated.

Centennial Year was the culmination of a period of cultural rediscovery for Quebec; but for English Canada it was an awakening. Expo and the year-long national celebrations gave Canadians a rare glimpse of themselves as a country. It was altogether the biggest national undertaking since the war, and with Expo's great success, English Canadians became aware of themselves as some sort of cultural entity. The festivities taking place all over the country, many spontaneously, sparked a renewal of interest in history and tradition that did not pass with the centennial itself. English Canada continued on with its cultural revival, producing more books, plays, paintings and songs for Canadian audiences over the next decade than were probably produced in the entire previous century. The burst of activity, moreover, was spread out around the country, involving many genres and many landscapes and touching many regional sensibilities. What made it all possible was the rather calculated determination of a generation of Canadian artists to stay in Canada to pursue their careers. Yet to reverse tradition — the old choice between poverty and exile — they had to invent some new means of publishing and performing their work. It was clear that the established institutions of élite and mass culture — theatres, publishers, arts councils and the like — tended to overlook local talent. As a consequence, some artists went into business for themselves. Others returned home from successful careers in the US or elsewhere to join the adventure. Very quickly it began to dawn on them that being a Canadian artist is in itself a political act. Economically speaking, on the bread-and-butter level, it meant competing with the continentally organized cultural industries to recapture part of the Canadian market for Canadian culture.

Since Centennial Year, this community of "cultural producers" has organized itself into professional and trade associations to represent its various interests and to push for legislative changes to foster an enterprise capable of taking root and standing on its own. Believing that while government action cannot create cultural development, it can certainly facilitate it, these groups have analysed their own situations and campaigned for radically new cultural policies that would recognize that our colonial condition is a prime obstacle to the adequate and proper distribution of Canadian culture to its public. In making their case for the preservation and support of cultural resources to both public and private sponsors, these associations have had a significant impact. The establishment of the Federal Cultural Policy Review Committee (the Applebaum-Hébert Committee) was a tangible result of their efforts.

By dint of ingenuity and perseverance, Canadian artists had succeeded, by the mid-Seventies, in establishing an indigenous network, parallel to the main roads of official culture (though on a smaller scale, of course) — a Sixties-type underground for Canadian culture. Moreover, they gradually found enthusiastic audiences for their work, showing that, when given the opportunity, Canadians are just as eager to share in the expression of their own culture as any other group of human beings. Movies like *The Apprenticeship of Duddy Kravitz* and *Who Has Seen the Wind*, which were both based on Canadian literary classics and which managed to get national distribution, broke box-office records. And Canadian audiences, with no help from Hollywood, have turned some of our artists into stars — Toller Cranston, Gordon Pinsent, Karen Kain, Gordon Lightfoot.

But because we find the major mass media channels under foreign occupation, it is practically impossible to foster a nation-wide familiarity with contemporary Canada and Canadian culture. The audiences for Canadian work are fragmented, localized. Canada's version of the Quiet Revolution is, of necessity, silent. However, as Margaret Atwood once remarked, the fact that Canadians may be unable to articulate their sense of national identity does not mean that it doesn't exist. Our situation has meant that very few of us are in the fortunate position of being able to experience our country as a whole, in all its astonishing variety.

In the same way, the movements for social change in Canada have been flung out across a broad expanse of territory and issues, making the results hard to perceive in any coherent shape. Several regions of the country have, like Quebec, experienced upheavals brought on by the abrupt and careless dictates of mid-twentieth-century industry: the outport resettlements in Newfoundland, the decline of the family farm in the West, the decimation of native communities and the assimilation of francophone communities outside Quebec.

But resistance to the conditions and contradictions of advanced capitalism is not unknown to Canadians, and here, too, we have observed citizens in the streets, in the courts, at city hall and in the myriad local coalitions and *ad hoc* committees that have sprung up to fight for people's rights and against bureaucratic mismanagement. Nor are the issues unrelated: native land claims; alternative energy systems; equal pay for work of equal value. If they seem diffuse, they do share certain political and philosophical principles: participation, conservation and the moral need for accountability to society as a whole on the part of all those who exercise power, whether private or public.

But whereas such struggles in Quebec have found a focus and common cause in the nation, combining into a political force strong enough to inspire politicians and move governments, this has not been the case in Canada. For one thing, Canadian nationalism got mired in the theory and practice of economic nationalism, with a distinct bias toward the fears and fortunes of industrial Ontario. Only lately has there been any

sign of the outlook broadening to encompass matters of social
and cultural significance or an understanding of Canada's
regional character.

More often than not, the moves for autonomy or local
determination in Canada have been understood by participants
and observers alike as regionalism — which is to say province-
building rather than nation-building. That spirit of independence so typical of the West, moreover, is usually fuelled by
some measure of anti-Ontario resentment; this, of course, has
a basis in real history and the long parade of "national"
policies, which have been little more than the will of Ontario
industrialists writ large. But when an outfit like the Canada
West Foundation, a lobby group funded by the four Western
provincial governments, corporations and businessmen, talks
with discreet relish about Western separatism, we know that
it is not the voice of the working poor of Calgary we are hearing
but the voice of Western free enterprise, which has ached for
so long to be free from Ottawa in order to make a few fast
bucks on its own with the Americans.

Nevertheless, we would be gravely mistaken to dismiss
regionalism just because it has been cleverly exploited by
provincial politicians and local élites. On the contrary, it is a
healthy sign of strengthening regional attachments, which
have altered the political climate in the Eastern and Western
provinces over the past fifteen years or so. The days when it
was possible to get elected promising more federal government
hand-outs are long gone. There is widespread disenchantment
with the Come-by-Chance approach to regional economic
development and a growing realization that self-reliance is the
key to lasting economic and social development. Small-scale
projects that can be integrated into existing activity are better
risks.

We would suggest further that there is a positive side to
regionalism that distinguishes it from provincialism — the
statism practised by provincial politicians — and from the crass
competition between disadvantaged regions for equalization
pay-offs. In a collection of provocative essays entitled *Radical
Regionalism*, George Melnyk proposes a new kind of
regionalism that, in his own region, would be rooted in the
landscape and history of the prairie, drawing on native and
immigrant experience while working for autonomy and greater
self-sufficiency for the region as a whole. Moreover, Melnyk's
regionalism does not set itself up as a rival movement to
nationalism; instead it implies a new way of conceptualizing

nationalism—one that draws strength from its regional roots, where southern Ontario might think of cultivating its own regional consciousness.

If, as Northrop Frye has said, painters and writers are not acts of God but come out of specific communities and are the individual points where these communities become articulate, we can recognize that the Canadian nation, following Quebec's example, has begun to find its voice. Like their Quebec counterparts, many Canadian artists have broken with the colonial attitudes of the past, asserting that the problem is not to "find" the Canadian identity, which already exists, but to make it visible. In this they have been inspired in a general way by the accomplishments of the artistic vanguard of the Quiet Revolution.

The long-term influence of this cultural or national expansion, however, is by no means assured; we cannot even be sure that ten years from now we will still be producing books, films or plays of our own, given the precarious state of Canadian cultural industries. Already some Canadian journalists who became cultural nationalists for a time in the Seventies are declaring that the movement was only a phase, a passing fad whose time has gone (so for them, presumably, it's back to American internationalism as usual). It is a problem that many dissenters have encountered with the news media, which follows events, not causes, and particularly not unresolved causes.

Nevertheless, we have proven in the last decade, Canadians and Quebeckers together, that the Canadian state is inhabited by two rich and vital societies that possess the talent and inventiveness to imagine their futures but lack the means of realization. Our consciousness industries may be colonized but, happily, the imaginative resources are not as yet.

The response of Canadian governments to the cultural situation of Canada and Quebec has been twofold: first, cultural affairs have been recognized as a legitimate area of public policy, although only in Quebec are they accorded much political importance. The call for a national cultural policy was first made when Gérard Pelletier was secretary of state, but four secretaries of state and many promises later, the master policy has yet to appear. The "Applebert" committee, appointed by the Conservatives and re-anointed by the Liberals, held public hearings over the summer of 1981 and published a report in 1982. It, too, failed to articulate a guiding principle for cultural policy beyond reaffirming the long-established tradition of keeping cultural agencies at arm's length from government.

Secondly, money has been spent in the short term to shore up Canadian production, preserving a "residual" Canadian capacity to publish our own books, make our own films, and so on, if only for appearance' sake. In the arts and the media, the picture is gloomily similar. Individual artists are awarded arts council grants, while little is done to ensure their work will ever be produced or distributed by the organizations of élite culture that drain off the bulk of public funds. Federal policy has been a policy by default, not by commitment, sanctioning a mass culture dominated by American imports and run by American corporations, on the one hand, and an élite culture, artificially sustained by transfusions of "international art" from abroad, on the other.

For its part, Applebert managed to write four hundred pages on Canadian culture without ever addressing this fact. Although it acknowledges the importance of Canadian-owned publishers to Canadian literature (which wouldn't exist as we know it, had the branch plants been left to do the job), the committee stops short of drawing the obvious conclusions about foreign ownership. In fact, one of the committee members, economist Albert Breton, went so far in his minority report as to suggest that grants to the cultural industries should be equally available to foreign-owned firms.

Nevertheless, the agitation and lobbying have had their effects. Nowadays, along with survival grants to the Canadian fringes, we have a good deal of nationalist rhetoric, proclaiming the desirability of healthy Canadian-owned cultural industries, especially from ministers in charge of cultural affairs. It is also true that the Applebert report recognized two very important facts: that "the largest subsidy to the cultural life of Canada comes not from governments, corporations or patrons but from the artists themselves, through their unpaid or underpaid labour"; and that the preoccupation with building buildings (the "edifice complex") has blinded policy-makers to the question of what goes on inside them. In the committee's words:

> We have come to believe that federal cultural policy must place a new emphasis on encouraging the best use of our concert halls, theatres, cinemas, galleries and airwaves for the presentation to Canadians of the finest works of Canada's own creative artists. If

we fail to make stimulation of our own creative imagination the heart of cultural policies, we will continue to live in a country dependent on the products of other cultures and we will never elevate life in Canada to a space essentially its own.

Ten years ago, talk like that was considered revolutionary. So perhaps we should consider that aspect of Applebert a victory. The trouble is, however, that Applebert didn't match its rhetoric with recommendations for action. It offered no new ideas, much less a strategy to pull us out of the impasse, and rejected protectionism out of hand in favour of merely encouraging everyone to do better. Particularly curious, given the history of Canadian film and television, was the proposal that the CBC and the NFB bow out of production and turn their facilities over to the private sector. Suggesting that we dismantle the only two stable sources of Canadian programming at a time when new technologies such as satellite broadcasting are set to deliver American culture in super-abundance seems quite deluded if not actually suicidal.

Canadian policy-makers have always proceeded on the assumption that American culture is an immutable fact of Canadian life; that Canadian cultural policy has to accommodate itself to American needs and demands before it can shape itself around them. In 1983, this means accepting the "open skies" policy the United States is promoting around the world; licensing more and more satellites and cable services (including private dish antennae) to bring in more and more American television signals, in the pious hope that this time we will finally hitch our wagon to the US stars. To do otherwise, we are told, is censorship.

Of course, what the accusation is meant to obscure is the facts of life: the political economy of Canadian broadcasting, which militates against original Canadian production and sanctions absolute disregard for the importance of one's own native culture. Experience has shown us that what is being defended so passionately is not, in reality, viewer choice — certainly not the option of choosing Canadian programs — but the divine right of Canadians to have as much American television as technology can deliver (which often means more than even most Americans get!) and of private broadcasters and cable companies to make a bundle delivering it. The new electronic media, including the processing and transmission of data, have the capacity to completely annihilate "what remains of a distinct Canadian culture, of its regional and other unique components and, in the final analysis, of an independent Canadian state." So saith the CRTC's chairman, John Meisel, in a 1981 lecture. Yet the chairman of another national institution, Rowland Frazee of the Royal Bank of Canada, in an article in *Chimo* titled "Best Friends, Whether We Like It or Not," admonishes us to resist protectionism, which he describes as "politically attractive and newsworthy." He says we should have the equivalent of an Auto Pact in information and communications, a Buy–North America act to achieve "freer trade in information as a step to opening up the world."

Concern about assimilation, such a vivid and immediate threat to francophone communities in North America, is usually mentioned in connection with French Canada, and it never seems to enter the heads of English Canadians to wonder how far their culture and society have already been assimilated. Americanization is talked about, and the American media are acknowledged to have an overwhelming influence in Canada; but how do we measure its advance? What statistics can chart its progress? Obviously the answers aren't ready to hand, but when we listen to arguments like Frazee's we may indeed be hearing the voices of assimilation, the people who can no longer differentiate between "them" and "us."

And so, Canadian cultural industries continue to live on the sidelines of the Canadian market, at the edge of financial insolvency. Only in Quebec do we find a government with a serious interest in cultural policy. And here, of course, the difference is the long- and well-understood connection between culture and survival. Accordingly Quebec was the first province to set up a ministry of cultural affairs, and since 1961 it has issued a number of major studies and statements on cultural policy: the Rioux commission on the teaching of the arts (1969); Jean-Paul L'Allier's Green Papers on communications (1972) and culture (1976); and Camille Laurin's White Paper on culture (1978). However, it is language legislation that has captured the limelight, with its steady evolution from Johnson's Bill 63 to Bourassa's Bill 22 to Lévesque's Bill 101.

Nevertheless, none of this has produced a strategy to overcome US domination of Québécois culture. Electing to pit its energies against Canadian domination without recognizing that this means American domination in most cases, the PQ boxed itself into the same position as its predecessors—doing battle with Ottawa for the little bit of room left over. On balance, Quebec governments over the years have asked for very little cultural change in their bargaining for a "greater measure of autonomy." Robert Bourassa's cultural sovereignty, despite the intonations of independence, could only have landed Quebec Ottawa's job of superintending the American pipeline, at best. The PQ so far have not advanced the argument much. Sovereignty-association would have given Quebec exclusive responsibility for communications and for the subsidy of traditional élite culture. Beyond that, the party has done very little rethinking or updating of previous Liberal policy. And everything else, mass culture and popular culture alike, is left to struggle on, with kind words and encouragement from Camille Laurin.

From this review of our relations with the United States, we could argue that Canada is the oldest, closest and most willing of America's colonies. Indeed, it is. Yet, if we are in that sense the most colonized, our position is not without privilege. We are not abject peoples; we have not been consigned to helpless impoverishment, illiteracy and social decay as have other colonial victims in the world. And Canada has achieved a degree of industrialization and a standard of living that most of the world envies. We act very much like an advanced capitalist society, and we indulge in some economic imperialism of our own to prove it. We have our own airlines and our own nuclear reactors, and we practise international affairs at the United Nations. Outwardly we are the model of a modern independent state. But it is a façade, and Quebeckers and Canadians have been taking it for real for too long.

Chapter 3

Culture and Empire

I

In the last two chapters we wrote about Canada and Quebec as two nations, and about their experience as two national communities, growing up in an affluent suburb of the American empire. Beginning as we all do with personal experience, we find lessons in the individual search for emancipation and self-knowledge that tell us something about the collective urge of a society to realize the same thing. Often disregarded yet essential to the process, both personal and collective, is the human imagination — the capacity to imagine a different person or society and to invent ways of bringing it about.

Let us now take a broader perspective and look beyond our own borders to the larger arena of dominance and dependence among countries — what some euphemistically call the balance of power. The so-called "expansion of interdependence" in a world ever more deeply divided by unequal opportunity is but a warning that the stakes for the powerful and the poor alike are escalating. We will focus our attention on the part played by culture in the exercise of political and economic power, examining culture's relationship to imperialism from several angles, the most obvious being the contribution of the transnational entertainment industry to the dissemination of American production systems, telecommunications systems and value systems around the world.

As we will argue, political and economic decisions even at

their most mundane carry a cultural attitude with them and have cultural and social consequences, whether acknowledged or not: economic and political activity has its cultural side, and by the same token, cultural activity has political and economic aspects. Considering the growing importance of information and information technology to the industrialized world, we ignore the conduct of our cultural lives at great peril, for the question of culture is fundamental. It lies at the heart of who we are and what we want to be.

In pursuing our discussion we will draw on the observations of others who have travelled this terrain before. Some of their names may be unknown to English readers — Jean Baudrillard, Pierre Rosanvallon and Cornelius Castoriadis, to name a few. Others, such as Sartre and Marcuse, though heroes to the counter-culture in the Sixties, are more widely known than they are read. But if we can generalize about the direction their thinking has taken, it is toward a fuller understanding of the cultural dimensions of society and of the role of technology and the imagery it disseminates. For many of these thinkers, the point of departure was disenchantment with the Marxism practised and proselytized by the Soviet Union.

Castoriadis, for example, came to appreciate from his experience in the Greek resistance that Stalinist politics, no less than fascism, is radically opposed to the project of "proletarian self-liberation." After the war, he emigrated to France, where he became a leading figure in the emerging anti-Marxist Left. Castoriadis was a member of the group Socialisme ou Barbarie ("Socialism or barbarism"), which published a journal of the same name from 1948 until just before the revolution in May 1968. Because of his position as a high-ranking official with OECD, he had to write under a pseudonym; only recently has he begun to use his own name.

At the heart of Castoriadis's argument is a rejection of traditional political theories, which treat the working class as a kind of inert object with practically no function and no responsibility in the revolution or in the shaping of a new society afterward. In this view, "the absurdity of all inherited political thought consists precisely in wanting to resolve men's problems for them, whereas the only political fact is this: how can people become capable of resolving their problems for themselves? [our translation]" The political ramifications of this perspective are explored in Chapter 4, but for the moment, we return to the original question of culture.

Because the word culture has many meanings and is at the

same time a part of everyday language, we should probably begin by setting down our own interpretation as precisely as possible. As yet, there is no commonly understood meaning evoked by the word culture as there is, say, with equivalent concepts such as education or economics; and so, writers on the subject have made a convention of prefacing all discussion with a definition of terms—an honest exercise, but one that nevertheless has compounded the confusion. Surveying the forest of definitions, however, we can detect three basic types. First and by far the most common is the definition that concentrates on what culture *is*, by enumerating the objects and activities that make it up. The lists run from the strict and narrow, which only admits "works of art," to the broad and loosely defined, which includes all manner of social activity—cuisine, sports, dress, language and so on.

The second kind of definition, implied in some of the more eclectic inventories, emphasizes behaviour and attitude more than the individual forms of cultural expression. It leans more to the anthropologist's than the art historian's view of the world, seeing culture as a system of social conventions and values that informs institutional as well as individual conduct. The outward manifestations of cultural evolution can still be read as a sequence of events and personal statements, but these only tell part of the story. In biology, as we know, ecology is the study that relates the habits and modes of life of living organisms to their physical surroundings. Likewise, the culture of human beings can be said to comprise the vast complex of relationships of individuals and groups to their social and physical surroundings. In 1975 a special Tribunal on Culture was convened in Montreal by a group of artists, publishers and film-makers to hear representations from the public on the conduct of the Ministry of Cultural Affairs, by then almost fifteen years old. Among the members of the research committee that conceived the project was *Parti pris* editor and poet Gérald Godin, who was to defeat Premier Robert Bourassa in his own riding of Mercier one year later (to become minister of immigration and cultural communities in the PQ government). The jury, chaired by Marcel Rioux, published its "Évidence" and "Jugement" in the fall issue of *Liberté*, commencing with this penetrating definition of culture:

> For many decades the word culture has been used
> by all the social sciences to designate a society's
> distinctive way of life. One can speak of the Iroquois

culture, of German, of Québécois culture, or of culture as an ensemble of institutions, values and practices that make one society distinct from the next. The French economist Jacques Attali has written, "In all societies the relationship of man to his environment and to other men is ruled by a collection of common representations, attitudes and behaviours that lends them a sense of belonging, over and above the immediate sense of language and culture." What we should remember here is that the notion of culture and the reality that surrounds it (and here most definitions agree) encompasses the combined behaviour of individuals and collectives in the political as well as the economic domain, in daily life as well as intellectual life. Culture—the world of values, images, signs and symbols—is manifest in the economy (defined as the production of goods and services) as well as in politics (defined as the organization of power). Dominant groups and classes tend to want to control symbolic production, which is the culture of a society just as much as its economic production. (our translation)

A third approach, pioneered by Europeans such as Sartre and Castoriadis, stresses the innovative, self-creative capacity of people and the collective imagination, or *imaginaire social*, which makes it possible for a people to surpass received knowledge and tradition. Without this vital element, societies would remain forever static.

Significantly, while this broader approach to culture has been absorbed into the mainstream of French thought and study in Europe and Quebec, it has had only a marginal influence in the English-speaking world. Among those disciplines that bother to concern themselves about culture at all, definition rarely strays beyond the simple and basically materialistic equation of culture with commodities. Moreover, the public attitude toward art and artists is remarkably different in the two linguistic communities. Critics here have lamented the fact, on more than one occasion, that the respect and pride invested by the Québécois in their artists and their culture is so rare a thing in English Canada. Bernard Ostry, the former deputy minister of the federal Department of Communications, for one, published an essay on culture and government policy that reproaches all Canadian governments save Quebec's for their permanently ingrained neglect of cultural policy.

True to form, when the Applebaum-Hébert Committee issued its discussion paper in 1980 in preparation for public hearings, it, too, yielded to the conventional English-Canadian myopia about culture, choosing to exclude the anthropological approach on the feeble pretext that because its mandate had to be limited, the definition of culture should be tailored to fit.

In the committee's conception, culture continues to be equated only with those pleasures and inessentials of life upon which the population spends its discretionary income. All the eloquent pleadings of the arts community notwithstanding, culture is still treated as a frill. For practical men of affairs and politicians who like to think of themselves as realists, culture falls into the realm of passion, which is to say it belongs to the privacy of personal life. Business and politics, on the other hand, are proper to the domain of reason, which they believe rules the "real world." On the podium, the powerful may speak in reverent tones about civilization and the quality of life; but in the boardroom, the only things that count are profit margins and technological prowess.

If we proceed with an understanding of culture that embraces all three definitions and also looks behind the materialistic and behaviouristic to the imaginative forces driving culture, we will open ourselves to some fascinating speculations about the state of our cultural health. We can make a comparison, for example, between culture and energy, for both are primary sources of change and development in contemporary society.

The German physicist Rudolf Clausius, renowned for his studies of the transfer of heat in matter, coined the term "entropy" some time ago to describe the process of steady degradation of energy that, according to some current theories of modern physics, is propelling the universe toward ever-greater disorder. Energy is becoming more and more inaccessible, increasingly to be found in forms that are awkward or difficult to utilize. Another eminent scientist, Erwin Schrödinger, refers to "the heat death of the universe," brought on by the exhaustion of usable energy sources and the lack of new techniques for exploiting what remains. Considering the mounting alarm about the rate with which Western civilization is using up energy, such a cosmological outlook could hardly be more appropriate.

The analogy between culture and energy may be more than a metaphor; parallels have been drawn in describing the properties of energy and information, and other similarities have already been demonstrated, at least in theory. If we can broadly define culture as a code that imposes order on the welter of information reaching individuals from the external world, we might also compare it to the organizing function of a computer program, which transforms raw data into intelligible bits of information. Call it what you will, the mechanism gives sense to reality, and without it human beings would be adrift in a bewildering sea of undifferentiated messages, where every event is as plausible and as probable as the next.

According to this conception, culture would seem to be moving in the opposite direction of energy—that is, not toward entropy and chaos, but toward greater order. Appearances, however, may be deceiving.

Culture, like energy, has many origins and many forms. Each of the multitude of cultures that have appeared on earth since the beginning of humanity has stood as the incarnation of a unique social occurrence, located within and developed out of a particular set of circumstances, but choosing from an infinite array of possibilities. Since antiquity, the world has known some cultures to be stronger than others, and some to display aggressive, domineering attitudes toward the people of other cultures. Empires have always exerted a cultural influence on subject territories and colonies and have usually sought to control their universe by imposing their own customs and laws on everyone, discrediting—if not destroying—other laws and other customs. One after another, these hegemonic cultures have come and gone, sometimes leaving entire continents to reconstruct local traditions and ways of life afterward.

In our time, American culture—that is, the culture of American commerce and consumerism—predominates throughout the West. Does it not seem as if the Europe of today, seat of so many defunct empires, has itself fallen under the spell of America? Yet when we talk of the American empire, it is clearly not one fashioned on previous models. Perhaps by dint of its enormous cultural influence, the United States is on its way to succeeding where bygone empires have failed, its secret being a highly developed technique of internal social co-option instead of overt coercion.

So even in relatively rich and stable places like Canada and Quebec, we hear the opponents of nationalism claiming that modern interdependence among nations supersedes the possibility of genuine independence and thus renders nationalism obsolete. They warn us that it would be foolhardy and probably futile to opt out of the empire just when space-age communications technology and mega-economics are creating new super-networks, capable of bring the entire world into instantaneous touch. Time and space evaporate before we can distance ourselves.

Yet from another perspective, we might be led to the opposite conclusion: that it would be foolhardy indeed to rush irrevocably into a pre-fabricated future without first examining the proposition that culture, like energy, could be finite and exhaustible, that perhaps in this domain, too, we have entered a vulnerable state. As with industrial development, we may be sacrificing the cultural equivalent of renewable energy for vainglorious dreams of high-tech power.

In other words, if it is true that we are evolving toward a single world-wide culture (Coca-Cola having penetrated the Bamboo Curtain), could we at the same time be moving toward a cultural as well as an energy shortage? Certainly the message of American corporate culture to the world is, explicitly and implicitly, that the American way of life is best for all mankind, and moreover, that this is progress. It may happen someday that we all do become Americans, but for the moment, those transnational American-style executives and businessmen, as they circulate from Hilton to Hilton, can still sample spectacles of native cultural exotica staged for the titillation and fancy of tourists. The Japanese can find plenty of monuments worth photographing, and tourism has become a profitable industry marketing picturesque relics of disappearing worlds. What tourism sells is the idea that cultural difference is mere entertainment.

So long as culture is thought of only as a product, the manufacturing and distribution systems — that is, the activities of providing and controlling culture — can be taken for granted. And, of course, the fact that in our economic system, the cultural industries are structured like other industries and share similar methods and means of operating is obscured. Furthermore, industry itself is seen as proper to the realm of economic culture.

Often what we remember most about another culture is its particular use of a technology. The Roman arch, the Spanish galleon and the Inuit igloo are symbols for entire civilizations. So today, American civilization is characterized by its most important tools: the automobile, the television and the computer. It is a civilization unique in history for the fantastic complexity of its technology and its reach into every facet of daily life and work. For many people, the pervasive power of technology—meaning both the systems and the institutions that run them—is the major social issue of our time.

Some think, and many believe, that the best way of saving our skins is not to reject American technology but to adapt it to our own needs. In this view, technology is understood as an assemblage of hardware (wires, motors and transistors), which is in itself innocent of any kind of prejudice or favour. Technology is neutral and can therefore accommodate itself to any social situation without affecting it *a priori*. Everything depends on how it's used.

Nothing, in fact, could be less likely. History shows that there is a strong correlation between the technology a society employs and what it decides to do with it—the kinds of cities it builds, who it trades with and so on. Lewis Mumford, the American anthropologist, has shown, for example, that big machines and big factories are concomitant with the rise of big corporations and big unions, and all of them relate to the establishment of monopolies.

The late shah of Iran, in modernizing his country American-style, overlooked this double-edged character of technology and thus failed to appreciate the shock wave that would be sent throughout Iranian society by massive injections of Western methods and machinery. It is through a similar misunderstanding of the interaction of technology, economics and politics that Lenin set his country on a course toward the grinding state capitalism that exists there today. Socialism, he wrote:

> is impossible without large-scale capitalist engineering, based on the latest discoveries of modern science. It is inconceivable without planned state organization which keeps tens of millions of people to the strictest observance of a standard of production .... [O]nly those who understand that it is impossible to create or introduce socialism without learning from the organizers of capitalism are worthy of the name Communist.

Lenin tried to resolve the contradiction between social production and private ownership by marrying German industrial techniques to a different production unit (the soviets and commune) and ended up with Communism. He also believed that technology can be borrowed with impunity.

The question for us, however, is whether the technology of corporate capitalism can be used for anything other than capitalist pursuits. Or to put it the other way around, can we, as members of an industrialized society, come up with some alternative technologies that will safeguard what is important to us from our past — our collective soul, so to speak? Can technology be humanized, or is it wishful thinking to suppose it can be adapted without a massive overhaul of life-styles and values?

Thus far, the experience of conservationists who have tried to design environmentally balanced households or businesses shows how difficult it is to achieve such harmony in the average urban setting. No doubt part of the allure of the back-to-the-land movement was the intuition that country living makes it easier to change living patterns from the ground up. Certainly we have learned that the way various elements of social activity are contingent upon one another means that a change in one vital part will sooner or later colour the whole fabric. We know that earthquakes and war send ripple effects through society, but neither of these phenomena can match the astounding chain reaction caused by, say, the automobile, which completely transformed the economy and culture of most of the world. Television now is doing the same thing, and its field of action is inside our minds.

The problem of energy supply that plagues the West poses yet another question about technology. Is it reasonable to assume, given the conditions industrialized societies have created for themselves, that we can continue along the same road and reduce energy consumption at the same time? To date, the warnings of authorities have resulted in almost nothing in the way of systematic conservation programs, and this could well be because they are proposing the impossible: to maintain the *status quo* while changing one of the basic elements that makes it tick. The absurdity of our system is that serious conservation (of water, hydro or gas) drives up utility prices, because volume drops and revenues diminish. The reaction of oil companies and governments to the 1973 energy crisis has not been to institute a strict husbanding of scarce reserves, but to do the very opposite. Furiously they have rushed ahead with the exploitation of existing resources, using higher prices and larger profits to finance exploration and development of exotic and dangerous new methods of energy production, extracting oil from the ocean floor under treacherous seas and electricity from nuclear reactors, creating toxic wastes. Instead of conserving, we are compelled to be forever searching after new repositories of energy. As the easily extractable reserves are used up, development costs spiral and so, too, paradoxically, does the amount of energy consumed in the processing of them.

Economists who have reflected on this paradox, like Vassily Leontieff and Robert Heilbroner in the United States, are not wrong in concluding that the solution to the energy crisis lies among the most fundamental values and ethics on which society is based — in short, on culture. The culture will have to change if conservation is to be achieved. There are many examples of groups and individuals willing to contemplate just that sort of radical, deep-seated change. And their example, encouraged by hard times and unemployment, has produced phenomena like barter exchanges and no-frills supermarkets. It has also led to environmentalists running for public office, as the Green Party did in the West German election of 1983.

In fact, understanding the environmental threat means that the postulates of industrial society, which have produced traditions and institutions of genius and positive purpose, nevertheless have led us into a cul-de-sac. Caught up in the instant, captive of the short term, it is hard for us to discern, let alone plan the necessary changes. Who dares today to predict interest rates or the price of oil? Being creatures of habit, we tend to go back to old formulae that once yielded results, without asking whether they could well exacerbate the situation at this stage. The automobile is supposed to transport people quickly from one place to another; yet when enough cars are crowded into a street, it is quicker to use a bicycle than to drive.

And, alas, war continues to be a favourite recipe for recharging a sagging economy. Fresh horizons, distant territories promising valuable raw materials and other riches have ever been a temptation too hard to resist. Rather than trimming life-styles or curbing excess profit, why not do a little prospecting in foreign regions where conquest may open up new markets? So much the better if it requires force, for that will boost the maufacturing and resource sectors. And what of the arms race, which has suddenly staged a come-back against the backdrop of a renewed cold war? As usual, even the smallest countries arm themselves with weapons purchased from the big powers, who are, for their part, armed to the teeth with the latest, fanciest, state-of-the-art issue.

Our own era has witnessed the spectacle of Russia hustling to catch up with the United States, and we have seen the results of the two superpowers doing battle with each other by proxy through smaller countries, sowing death and destruction wherever their influence runs. Each side takes its body count and rejoices when the balance of devastation tilts in its favour.

Without delving into the similarities between Russian state capitalism and American private capitalism, it is apparent that they are based on simliar systems of production and industrial development. Marx himself had high praise for the middle classes' ability to develop production, and it was Lenin who urged Communists to emulate "American efficiency." This tenet of Marxism, which prizes the techniques of advanced capitalism, is one of the few faithfully followed by the Soviet Union today, which has produced its own huge, heavy-handed and centralized brand of bureaucracy. As with their armaments, the two empires have a way of imitating each other in their general social characteristics. Trapped in the escalation of terror, neither side can afford to backtrack for fear of inviting the other to advance. And sooner or later everyone is forced to join their march toward nuclear war.

It is, of course, all too easy to conjure up terrifying images of cruelty and waste. However, our purpose here is not despair, but to search for a way out of the labyrinth. So we return with hope to our road map and continue.

II

An instructive way of approaching the phenomenon of culture is by analogy to nature's intricate and delicate balancing act, known as ecology. As with energy, we are on familiar ground because of the predictions of man-induced disaster popularized (if we can use that term) in recent years by environmentalists. Suffice it to reiterate the truth that observers from Rachel Carson to the present have forced upon us: that unbridled industrial growth and development of the forces of production have ruptured the equilibrium of the forces of nature, and we are most likely heading toward catastrophe.

The mechanisms of consumption and production are now so completely enmeshed in ordinary life, individuals and groups so caught up in the thousands of ties that bind them to the present situation, that one can only wonder whether these machines can be stopped before they lay waste to humanity. We are learning the hard way that nature is not infinitely exploitable, that we can permanently alter and destroy parts of the physical world and then live to see the effects spin themselves out over generations with dreadful retribution. To cite two examples close to home: the outbreak of Minamata disease that has scourged native Indians living and fishing along the mercury-polluted waters of the English and Wabigoon rivers in northern Ontario; and Reye's syndrome, a disease usually fatal to children that has been attributed to chemical agents in insecticides used to control the spruce budworm in the forests of New Brunswick. The catastrophe that sooner or later is bound to overtake us — the energy crisis being but one instalment of it — could mean the exhaustion of the planet's accessible resources. We have already seen the extinction of many species of animals; the appearance and proliferation of epidemic diseases caused by damage and pollution inflicted against nature and ourselves. And out there in space, the litter of man-made objects already exceeds four thousand pieces (soon to be joined by nuclear wastes, no doubt).

As long as industrial safety was thought of only in terms of direct injury to workers, the owners had little to worry about. In the old days the question of working standards could be confined to labour negotiations, kept out of the courts and the glare of publicity. Personal safety, so far as the management and directors of the company were concerned, was a moot point anyway. People could always move to healthier neighbourhoods. If pressed, you could build taller smokestacks to transport pollution to the upper atmosphere. The only trouble with that was it came down as acid rain. Pollution, especially the toxic variety that human industrial society produces, can't be "burned, bashed and buried" like tin cans in the woods. Now that we have invented a pollution that attacks whole cities, continents and oceans, it's everybody's business. Breathing itself can be fatal: no one can escape. The political problem of waste disposal is now acute.

And after discovering that modern man has invented devastating ways of dirtying the ecosphere, the populace is also awakening to the possibility that we may have found equally insidious methods of poisoning ourselves with the processing and chemical additives upon which the modern food industry depends. If man's ambition in extending his domain over nature has been the improvement of human life, it is hard to fathom why societies continue to comply with this assault on nature, knowing what the research (even research done to find better ways of mastering nature) foretells and seeing the evidence in front of our very eyes that the environment is falling apart.

People have been aware for decades that nature is being

squandered. Today we promote conservation and clean up oil spills. But even those inclined to conserve at home may be turning a blind eye to destruction happening abroad. People are more readily prepared to protest a chemical dump being put into their neighbourhoods than they are to renounce the system that produces the toxic wastes in the first place. Cynics might well imagine that a profitable pollution clean-up boom could end up creating a new industrial sector with a vested interest in continuing pollution. For the moment we can well wonder whether the clean-up side is gaining any ground at all. What becomes apparent, though, is the fact that control and manipulation of the environment goes hand in hand with control and manipulation of people; all of nature, human beings included, tends to become an instrument for the accumulation of wealth.

Those expecting to find any difference in the way socialist countries deal with nature are in for a disappointment, as the same ideology of technology and the same idea of industrial progress holds sway there, too. Industrial development implies the extension of control over human society. People have to be organized to form both a labour force and a market of consumers willing to buy what it produces. Since the *raison d'être* of the enterprise is growth—of power, profits and the gross national product—sooner or later states and corporations are tempted to extend their exploitation to other territories and other peoples as well.

While we in the West like to think that the influence exerted by the United States around the world is less oppressive and less violent than the Soviet Union's, the record shows that it, too, wreaks havoc on smaller and traditional cultures. Leaving aside the murky history of US government involvement in the internal politics of, say, the Middle East or Latin America, the mere presence of US corporations doing business has proven to have enormous and unambiguous effects on host societies. We are familiar with the consequences of US military action in Vietnam, yet the evening news scarcely reported the tremendous dislocation inflicted on Vietnamese society by the arrival of thousands of American GIs, with their cultural habits in tow and enough money to transform Saigon's economy. In order to count the final cost of that war, cultural disruption will have to be tallied along with the physical and environmental damage. Who can say which, in the long run, has been more devastating? For it is when a society loses its cultural fibre that it is at its weakest and most receptive to political and social manipulation. Considering this, we can appreciate that in its pursuit of cultural domination, the United States has taken the methods of imperialism to new levels of sophistication.

Through the long and varied history of empires, we can discern several phases. In ancient times, imperialism was primarily military: conquest was enforced by fire and the sword, and colonies were bound by the rule of the centralized authority. In the sixteenth century, when Portugal and Spain began trading around the world, opening up banks to facilitate the process, the economic aspects became ascendant, although political domination clearly followed hard on the heels of economic exploitation. Back home, colonialism was promoted as missionary work. Europeans had a duty not only to civilize the "heathen savages," as theologians called them, but to save them from Original Sin and themselves, by bringing them the true Christian religion — teaching them how to live and how to pray. But this is not to say that there weren't problems. For instance, it was difficult to undertake a just war so long as the natives were willing to let the foreigners in to trade and preach as they wished. What Spain and Portugal invented was a way of acquiring the booty of war without always having to fight for it. When Holland, England and France in turn took to empire-building, their monarchs chartered private companies to organize and carry out the conquest and exploitation. In this period, deculturation of local peoples happened in diverse ways — sometimes by outright extermination — but usually the clash of cultures itself would be sufficient to bring on such disequilibrium that the colonized society was not able to recover.

In the seventeenth century, military force evolved into an almost purely economic arrangement called mercantilism, whereby the mother country held exclusive rights over all commercial transactions within the colony. In England the Covenant Act of 1660 was explicit in the matter: "No merchandise, no product can be taken from the colonies except on English ships, or ships built or belonging to the colonies except on pain of confiscation." Under such conditions, only a limited segment of the indigenous population need actually come into direct contact with the colonizers; the vast majority were left to live out their lives as they always had. (Such, for example, was the lot of the *habitants*, ancestors of the Québécois, who were the first white settlers to create an indigenous society in North America.) With the close of the eighteenth century and the dawn of the industrial age, when the French Revolution was throwing Europe into confusion, domination abroad had to be reoriented. The old mercantilism no longer responded to the expansionist aims of the powerful. In this period, we see the launching of great colonial empires of the British and the French. Now it became a matter of accumulating territories to do business with—that is, to sell manufactured goods to and take raw materials from.

The First World War jarred loose the hold of these regimes; the Second World War delivered the *coup de grâce*. In the meantime, the United States had taken first place as the world's biggest and most advanced industrial power. The twentieth century has become the era of the American empire, the Americans continuing the tradition of their predecessors with little fundamental change. It is a kind of super-imperialism that usually dispenses with the preliminaries of military or political conquest, effecting subjugation through economic activity—sweetened, as we know, by the material conveniences it provides. Economic domination, once achieved, is held in place by cultural domination. Not that military, political and economic forces don't come into play any more, but we could say they are made palatable by the ideology of world capitalism and its conception of "the good life."

The period after the Second World War was characterized by what has been called the internationalization of economics, accompanied by a measure of political integration achieved through a series of new transnational organizations (such as the UN and the European Common Market) as well as through international treaties.

In traditional class analyses (of Canadian or any other society), there is usually a good deal to be said about the support system that helps keep one dominant group in power. A system of legitimization accompanies the exercise of power. Likewise in the international context, imperial powers promote whichever ideology best explains and justifies their continued purpose. It may well be that the most effective weapon in the empire's arsenal these days is not the Backfire bomber or the Cruise missile but the transistor radio and the tools of ideological warfare. For all its innocuous and glitzy exterior, the American cultural influence takes dead aim at all local cultures, especially their political and economic aspects.

Watching this happen, we can sense that as industrial society grows, it is destroying not only the physical heritage of the universe but the cultural heritage of the human race as well. The strategy of mass marketing, which is based on the standardization of production, is to simplify demand. In order for manufactured goods to be distributed everywhere, large numbers of individuals have to want the same things. Demand must exist as widely as possible, and if it doesn't, it must be stimulated. The absolute ideal of any marketing operation is to locate, or if necessary create, a huge and homogeneous band of like-minded clones.

Whether they like to admit it or not, the managers of our economy are really in the culture business, promoting and selling life-styles that utilize their products. This is the real purpose of the commercial, though the film or program accompanying it is usually part of the selling job, too. At home, at work or in transit, we are seldom out of sight or sound of an advertisement of one sort of another. Is it any wonder that most traditional cultures, in the face of such sophisticated and powerful techniques, seem condemned to wither like plucked wildflowers?

But we should not fool ourselves that it is only the natives or "ethnics" who are affected in their isolated backwaters. All of us are threatened, especially those millions of us who have migrated to the comfort and order of urban living. Certainly, we in Canada have firsthand experience of the after-effects of cultures colliding, and we have witnessed the pernicious influence of European contact on native cultures. Our generation may have made some effort to halt the erosion, yet it continues unwilled and unabated. But while it may be easy for southern Canadians to grasp how the wholesale importation of southern television is incongruous with the way of life in the north, their own situation, ironically, is no different in kind. Southern Canada—which is to say, most of our population—has been flooded with imported US television programming for years. Would we not be guilty of arrogance, ignorance or both, if we assumed that our culture is hardier, more firmly rooted than those integrated, self-sufficient and often sophisticated native societies that flourished on this continent for centuries?

Of course, modern capitalism centres itself in large cities, where skyscrapers, expressways and billboards have become clichés the world over, and we should naturally expect cultural influence to concentrate there along with money and power. True, urban centres are often highly cosmopolitan, accommodating great diversity and even eccentricity, and true, there is a staggering array of cultural activities available. Nevertheless, city life tends to obliterate the material and social basis of customs and traditions of earlier, less mechanized times, and we are now able to find these only in small towns and outlying communities.

III

To continue the discussion of culture — as the compendium of values, ideas and knowledge acquired by an individual through a lifetime — we can recognize that cultural information reaches us from three sources, which can easily be recognized by examining one's everyday experiences. Generally speaking, cultural activity takes the form of the fine arts, the mass media and the rather more haphazard form of everyday life, at work, at home or in the street.

The mass media, of course, constitute the most conspicuous of our cultural networks. They are everywhere, up to the minute (or seem to be so) and immediate. Distinct from this is capital-C Culture, the culture of the "cultivated," which in Canada and Quebec and other Western nations is associated with certain artistic forms: ballet, the opera, painting, theatre, orchestral music and occasional works from the mass media when they conform to an exclusive aesthetic — for example, "art" films or photographs. Together, the fine arts derive from the cultural traditions of the Western world going back to ancient Greece. Not only are their forms inherited from European monarchies or aristocracies but, as we've said, the function of the fine arts is still manipulated by a statistically small élite and tends to reflect its interests. As mass culture is for the masses and of very general appeal, élite culture is for the élite, and its tastes are correspondingly restrictive. Mass and élite culture have this in common: they involve formalized and institutionally recognized specialists who produce objects or spectacles for a passive, paying audience.

Very often the catalogue of cultural activity ends here, ignoring the huge amorphous world of popular culture, which everyone participates in by virtue of belonging to the human race. We shall call it popular culture not because it enjoys the huge audiences of television or rock music, but because it is what *people* do. Popular culture tends to be traditional, amateur and spontaneous; by its nature, it refers to the immediate environment. But it differs from what museum curators and anthropologists have called folk culture: artifacts that have been separated from a live tradition to be put on public display and held in reserve for scholarly study. Popular culture is still part of everyday life, in the village, the neighbourhood or the clan. It consists of home-made meals, music, festivals and ceremonies. To illustrate the point, the National Museum of Man recently returned to a West Coast Indian community some of the artifacts confiscated from their ancestors at the time the potlatch was outlawed. These objects are now to be housed in a local community centre. They will rejoin a living cultural tradition — albeit one that has changed enormously over fifty years — and once again they will be used. As the centre's co-ordinator put it, "Indians don't go to museums." Popular culture is a conveyor of collective wisdom, skills, remembrances and history down the generations, and as such it is the wellspring and creative source for organized culture.

For its part, élite culture is the most highly specialized (and the most expensive) form of culture. It exists apart from the mainstream of life, taking place during "leisure time" in specially designated locations where the plush and marble interiors are redolent still of old aristocracies. From this vantage point, the doyens of élite culture set themselves up in judgment over supposedly lesser forms of culture, assuming guardianship over the Ark of the Covenant — truth, beauty and excellence. In doing so they also arrogate to themselves the job of separating art from the general cultural chaff — certifying it, as it were. If mass culture's primary purpose is commercial, that of the fine arts can be said to be the pursuit of excellence. Such an ideology tends to marginalize all culture, labelling culture itself superfluous beside the extremely serious work of society, where culture itself is mythologized as art, the mass media as entertainment and everything else as folklore.

The penetration of the media into daily life has profoundly affected our ways of socializing. Many traditional pastimes that used to bring people together to make music, fashion their tools and tell their own stories have vanished. Sometimes remnants are ritualized into performances or assembled into exhibitions for others. Today the Ukrainian choir performs on the stage of the school auditorium when once everybody joined in singing around the kitchen table on Saturday night. This is not to say that all cultural change is bad or unnatural. Old customs will die and new ones arise to take their place; culture is not static, if it is alive. Nor are we going to suggest turning back the clock or shutting down television. But we do have to recognize the fact that the culture of capitalism favours spectator culture, culture that demands the minimum creative input from the audience and promotes the disuse of the older spontaneous, self-made activity.

One salient characteristic of popular culture, as compared with the other categories, is its blurring of the rigid distinction between performer and audience, between production and consumption. Organized culture, following the lead of industry, breeds specialization. The pattern is familiar and repeats itself endlessly; in health care and education, for instance, the responsibility once shared by families and communities have been transferred to professionals, causing the skills and knowledge in these areas to fall out of general use. How many urban Canadians could hold a candle to Susanna Moodie, were roughing it in the bush ever to become necessary again? How long could Galveston, Texas, survive without air conditioning, or Winnipeg without central heating in winter? And how little we know today, as individuals, about growing food or making the tools and implements to clothe and shelter ourselves. The curious fact about most technical advances is that old skills die out as people become dependent on new conveniences. While providing cleaner and more comfortable living conditions, technology does not make people individually more self-sufficient within the natural environment. The point is that along with "development" comes a degradation and displacement of skills.

In many countries citizens have begun demanding that the massacre stop, that governments and communities put their efforts into planning development democratically so that a way can be worked out to reconcile the new with the old, to integrate post-industrial society without allowing it to ravage every other culture it comes into contact with. At the same time, many more people are consciously conserving and, in some cases, relearning old skills and crafts.

Yet while the guardians of the *status quo*, governments and captains of industry alike, are loath to admit the destructiveness of Western civilization, there have been disruptive reactions from unexpected sources. Old and venerable European nations thought to have been assimilated long ago (happy to parade in national dress on holidays, genuflecting to a scarce-remembered past) have undergone a resurgence. In Scotland, Ireland and Wales, in Corsica, Brittany, the Basque country and Catalonia, movements have materialized, boldly calling for autonomy or self-government if not outright independence. Frequently these national claims have been based on language differences (in relation to the central power), although, as in the case of

Scotland, this is not always so. In some international circles, Quebec is included on that list of independentist movements, and although the Quebec situation has certain unique aspects, there are interesting similarities.

The first is very general and dates back to the beginning of the Sixties, when turbulence arose over the national question. Bewildered English Canadians kept asking, "What does Quebec want?" In Europe, the same thing happened to national groups whose demands were not primarily economic in nature. As with other movements, the answer came gradually in Quebec; Quebeckers were moving in the direction of gaining the necessary power to conserve and develop themselves as a complete society, and the discovery led Quebeckers to the realization that culture is an all-encompassing phenomenon and functions at the very centre of society. The word culture was no longer reserved for privileged people; it burst onto the public stage and into political debate. The change can be briefly demonstrated by three examples.

At the outset of the Quiet Revolution, a ministry of cultural affairs was established in Quebec. The adjective "cultural" in the name derives its meaning from the root sense of "cultivating" land, and signifies, figuratively speaking, the cultivation of the spirit through the study of arts and letters: culture as a refinement. But immediately a kind of hierarchy among citizens is implied, in that some individuals could be said to be cultivated while others could not. Like its counterparts in other provinces, the Ministry of Cultural Affairs in Quebec took as its immediate goal the encouragement of the "fine arts." In this sphere, culture obviously has a different meaning than it does in the context of political movements.

With the appearance of the word "bicultural," coined in 1963 when Lester Pearson set up the Royal Commission on Bilingualism and Biculturalism, the meaning shifts again. And then we find it used in another sense when the premier of Quebec talked about Quebec's "cultural sovereignty" in the early Seventies. Nevertheless, there is a common thread in the two terms, deriving from a broader meaning than the old notion of cultivating the spirit through the appreciation of art. In both slogans there is also a suggestion that indeed there are two cultures functioning in Canada, paralleling the two main language groups. Obviously, Premier Bourassa wasn't proposing actual political sovereignty for Quebec; he was only staking a claim for provincial authority over Quebec's culture, which

Prime Minister Pearson had just officially recognized. So what did cultural sovereignty actually mean?

Though affirming that Quebec possesses a distinct culture, Bourassa clearly meant that it would still remain a province politically dependent upon Canada and economically dependent on Canada and the United States. For his part, Prime Minister Trudeau's response was to insist that sovereignty is indivisible, meaning that a state must retain sovereignty in all spheres or risk compromise. For Trudeau, cultural sovereignty was a contradiction in terms. The Montreal Tribunal on Culture concurred. But more to the point, it exposed cultural sovereignty as a sham insofar as it suggested that it would actually affect Quebec's sovereignty in some way. To Rioux, Godin and the others, it was nothing more than a political placebo to help inure Quebeckers to their economic and political subjugation.

Of course, Trudeau's logic on the subject took him down quite another path. Quite simply, he reasoned, if there is one state, one economy and one nation, then there can only be one culture or society. The wisdom of the B & B Commission, which had stated in the last sentence of its preliminary report of 1965 that "the negotiations between Canada and Quebec must involve the totality of the *two societies* which co-exist in Canada [emphasis added]," was swept aside; and in 1968 we were given multiculturalism instead.

The ruse fooled no one. To the tribunal, it revealed "the true Canadian reality, that Lord Durham's final solution [assimilate French Canadians into the English majority] has never really been abandoned by Canadian governments." Multiculturalism represented the trivialization of culture.

> Ethnic minorities have the right to their cultural traits, adding a bit of colour and life to the grey Canadian reality. What could be more engaging than a Ukrainian dance, an Eskimo sculpture, an Indian head-dress, an Italian restaurant or a German beerfest. Minorities can be piously encouraged to conserve their culture, and French Canadians can continue to assemble around a hearty meal of pork and beans. There are even federal grants available to keep all this multiculturalism going.

Furthermore, the tribunal took the position that although economics, politics and culture can be taken one by one for analytical purposes and separated into portfolios for political purposes, they are not experienced this way in real life. "Contrary to classic liberal doctrine, there is not a part of a person that is economic, another part political and another part cultural; rather, there is only a single personality, which envelops all these realities at once."

By supposing that a society comprises various elements that are interdependent, we have to ask what importance should be attached to culture and why, in our time, it should be seen as subsidiary to politics and economics. Because culture involves symbolic phenomena that are not as tangible as cabbages and kings, we tend to forget that political and economic institutions are themselves legitimized and upheld by ideals and values, though these may well be unspoken. The paradox is that in our society, the cultural factor is downplayed precisely because our particular cultural outlook gives priority to economic and political matters. Obliviousness to the cultural dimension is the hallmark of our civilization.

Since the independence movement came to prominence in Quebec, all aspects of Quebec society have been thrown open to inspection. The Parti Québécois government, professing that culture is less a commodity to preserve than a human resource to develop, set up alongside the superministry of economic development a superministry of cultural development. And culture, type-cast before as so much decorative icing on the cake, is now being thought of as the medium binding the whole confection together. Quebeckers have come to realize that conditions of political and economic dependence are also a threat to their culture. Why would Quebeckers struggle as they have if they were not convinced that their culture is different from that of Americans and Canadians? If culture were non-essential, they would have melted into the North American pot long ago.

Assimilation can and does take place imperceptibly, over time. In Quebec and in Canada, language has often marked the frontier; loss of French — that is, the conversion to English of formerly French-speaking households — is used to measure the rate of assimilation. Language is a natural bulwark to a culture's integrity, though it is by no means the only one.

But how in the world does one measure a population gradually adopting new, perhaps foreign, values as it abandons the old ones? For the most part, the process is invisible; we can only see the symptoms in plain view after it is too late. It is possible to say, however, at least in theory, that a culture is dead the day its members — the bearers of that culture — are submerged in an alien collectivity with its own set of mental structures, to the point of being unable to interpret what they borrow according to any self-generated cultural code. Deculturated people have difficulty creating original solutions for themselves and making decisions in their own best interests; eventually they lose the means and even the reason to survive as a distinct group.

As we have noted, the assimilation of English Canada by the US is not often taken very seriously. It is as if Canadian politicians all agreed with Robert Bourassa that we have "to choose between cultural sovereignty and our standard of living"—and that the choice is self-evident. The middle classes, in any case, take it for granted that standard of living is the ultimate measure of a society; though there are Canadians throughout the country who aren't very impressed with what it has achieved so far.

And it is no doubt due to a shared linguistic heritage that the border between Canada and the US has always been so porous. English-speaking Canadians move with facility and familiarity within American culture, and who can say whether this in itself has not been an attraction for American businessmen who find it expedient, not to mention profitable, not to have to distinguish between this country and the US. The irony of our situation is that when putting their case to English Canadians, Quebeckers have more often than not been addressing some of the world's most assimilated people, and among the most oblivious to the fact. A psychiatrist would have to wonder if the fear of Quebec nationalism were not mixed up in some way with a deeper fear of examining the other relationship—the one with the United States—in the same light. If a quantum leap forward in national consciousness on English Canada's part is needed, we can rest assured it won't be inspired by government ad campaigns. And it won't be inspired, either, by a prime minister who talks about Canadians' sense of commitment to their country as if it were a matter of will-power.

For Quebeckers wishing to work out a new association with Canada, inside or outside Confederation, that consciousness will be crucial, for otherwise negotiations will go forward only with great difficulty, with both sides speaking across an ideological as well as a linguistic divide. Without a parallel move on Canada's part toward assuming nationhood, there is a diminishing basis for mutual understanding. The virtue of a "yes" victory in the Quebec referendum for English Canada would have been that, in being compelled to respond to Quebec as a collectivity, Canada might have begun to think and act more like a nation. There may yet be other circumstances to force our consciousness ahead. (The Reagan administration has already helped by its frankly imperialist policies in Latin America.)

Meanwhile are there not alliances to be made, do we not have common cause, in resisting further encroachment from America Incorporated? To be sure, so long as Quebeckers are struggling with Ottawa for national independence, it may be unrealistic to expect them to open up the battle on another front. But even if resistance to American influence could well be the best argument of all for association with Canada, it is not at all clear to Quebeckers that the majority of Canadians are prepared to commit themselves to such an endeavour. And furthermore, it seems to them that in the short term, the national question is unlikely to surface on the political level at all in Canada, given that the business and political leadership is so much a part of the American alliance. ·

At the moment, the nationalist movement in English Canada appears to be scattered and diffuse. It seems to exist in unofficial and definitely extra-parliamentary habitats, and even some of the strongest voices in the national debate in English Canada are unknown in Quebec or, as in the case of a household word like Pierre Berton, unknown for their active involvement in cultural politics and the cause of strengthening Canadian culture.

To illustrate the striking discrepancy between Canada and Quebec in this respect, we can compare the contribution of post-secondary education to the national life in the two cultures. From the perspective of many Quebeckers, Canada is severely handicapped in this critical area.

In Quebec, teachers in the so-called "soft" subjects of philosophy, the humanities, social sciences and the arts have always been predominantly Québécois, and sensitized, one way or another, to Quebec's national question. Whatever their individual political opinions, the strength of the national feeling in the community at large has prompted academics and professors to acknowledge it. It has always been understood that before aspiring to international recognition (as a scholar or a nation), one must have a beginning, a point of departure, a frame of reference that only comes with an understanding of one's milieu. Non-Québécois teachers in universities and CEGEPs have never been numerous, but those who have come and stayed tend to become rather enthusiastically pro-Québécois over the years. This has not been the case in Canada.

On the contrary, as the Symons inquiry into the teaching of Canadian studies at Canadian universities reported in 1976, the presence of non-Canadian professors in large numbers on university faculties has contributed to the neglect of Canadian curricula. In Symons's words: "Few countries pay so little attention to their culture as Canada." The neglect, whether out of indifference or antipathy, has meant that Canadian universities are failing to train young Canadians to deal with uniquely Canadian problems in the sciences, professions and the arts.

> Many scholars and administrators at Canadian universities have adopted or accept the attitude that Canada is not a sufficiently interesting subject for study and research. Going further than this, some obviously feel that Canadian problems, events and circumstances are almost by definition of only second-rate importance.

Though the inquiry's survey included Quebec institutions, it was clear, even before work was begun, that the problem was really an English-Canadian one; and though delicately referred to as de-Canadianization, the real issue was (and is) Americanization.

In some universities, whole departments are virtually American colonies, and many Americans who have come here continue to live and work as if they had never left home. American methods and American trends are closely followed, and Canadians feel compelled to imitate the Americans if they wish to rate academically. Obviously, hiring practices favouring non-Canadians and non-Canadian qualifications are part of the vicious circle. Although the academic community prides itself on an allegiance to "excellence," standards by which such a thing is judged have to come from somewhere and, like all evaluations, are grounded in some culture or other. In reality, when such a cultural bias is not acknowledged, the way is open for discrimination, and Symons found ample evidence that Canadians and Canadian studies were being discriminated against at Canadian universities. Some US sociologists on Canadian faculties, he recounted, "were even forthright enough to tell the commission that they would not hire Canadians because (as they said) once one hires a few, then they will be pushing for more and more."

The dramatic expansion of colleges and universities in the Sixties, often advanced as the explanation for the imbalance of foreigners on Canadian faculties (particularly in the social sciences and fine arts, where the percentages range from sixty per cent to eighty per cent), cannot account for the fact that in Quebec the proportions are exactly the reverse. Symons saw the difference reflected in curricula. Canadian scholars, unlike their Quebec counterparts, have not taken their own country and history to be central to their field of inquiry; they do not look upon their task as being, in part, to help expand Canadian experience, bringing their special insight and knowledge to bear on contemporary life in Canada.

The Symons report is a fascinating historical document because it records one of those rare occasions when English Canadians took off the rose-coloured glasses long enough to look at the American influence in their midst and see how it might be affecting their own society. It is a study of the colonial mentality at work, and at the same time illustrates how American academics here have been allowed and encouraged to act as cultural missionaries. To the puzzlement of most Quebeckers, this critical issue has not yet been resolved. Although a follow-up report done for the secretary of state in 1981 indicates some progress in the number of Canadian studies courses offered, the general attitude of the academic community has scarcely improved. Canadians-first hiring practices are still anathema in most quarters and are still denounced as infringements on academic freedom.

There is no disputing that education is a society's link with the future and that in a very real sense, to lose control of it is to lose control of one's destiny. Certainly the imposition of foreign standards in education is one of the most debilitating features of colonization. As Frantz Fanon points out, the imperial standard — the language of the colonizer — is imposed as if it were universal, reducing everything, including all the best the colony has to offer, to perpetual inferiority.

IV

Because Canadians and Quebeckers have ringside seats in the global theatre of US enterprise, it seems to us that we have a special responsibility to bear witness, not just to save our own souls, but to document how US imperialism, even at its least differentiated and most benevolent, is hell-bent on the destruction of the manifold endowments of all humanity.

What do we really mean when we say that cultural domination may be the most highly developed stage of imperialism — the crowning achievement of previous imperialisms? To begin with, cultural domination does not happen unless the political, economic and technological factors are propitious. In describing the three historical phases of imperialism, we have indicated that even if the method of exploitation involves mainly military or economic techniques, the effects are always multiple, the economic spilling over into the political and cultural spheres and so on. There are instances on record, for example, where the spread of European goods was enough to traumatize indigenous people in areas where whites had not yet penetrated — the objects sometimes possessing no other value than their association with powerful strangers.

In the final analysis, cultural imperialism reaffirms and supports other forms of imperialism. But it is in itself the most insidious form, because of its capacity to erode identity, replacing the values and customs of the dominated with those of the dominator. It becomes a servo-mechanism — self-administered and self-perpetuating — whereby the colonized come to desire the invading values for themselves. Cultural imperialism assaults the host culture's most vulnerable core: its knowledge and awareness of itself, its very consciousness. When the empire is inside people's heads, there may be no need for gunboats.

Raymond Williams, writing about twentieth-century communications, has argued that the determining factor in the development of broadcasting since the Fifties in the non-Communist world has been the expansion of the American communications system. Initially developed for domestic use only, its evolution eventually meant penetrating broadcasting systems in all other available countries. So we see the transition from what were originally national or state-controlled sound broadcasting systems to what are now predominantly commercial and privately controlled television institutions governed by distant and unaccountable authorities (the multinational corporations).

This, Williams says, has to be understood as the consequence of a "planned operation from the United States." However, we should remember that some of the countries he is talking about here are France, Britain and Germany, which have well-established national broadcasting systems and well-developed film (and television) production industries. They are not, in other words, neophytes. Still, as Williams describes it in *Television, Technology and Cultural Form*:

> What surfaces in one country after another as a local argument, and quickly and pervasively described as a choice between "state monopoly" and "independent broadcasting", is in the overwhelming majority of cases, a put-up job by American interests, their local associates and the powerful international advertising companies.

The one-dimensional society, as Herbert Marcuse dubbed America of the Sixties, is cumulative and addictive, programmed to go on consuming other societies until it succeeds in reproducing itself everywhere. Of course, Marcuse understood that mass culture is created not by chance but by rigidlv defined and controlled formulae; its purpose is to amuse and romanticize while it propagandizes American power. Whatever the inconveniences of dependence, they are hidden beneath delicious images depicting life in the imperial metropolis as freedom and opportunity incarnate, where all human dreams can be realized and all desires fulfilled.

American culture comes in every colour of the rainbow and in breath-taking abundance, but it is governed nevertheless by strict laws dictated by economies of scale and centralized production, which prize uniformity and repetition, not diversity. In reality, consumer choice is far more limited than the illusion created by advertising. Planned obsolescence taps the genius of modern engineering to find ways of shortening the life span of goods to keep the consumer consuming; but it does not mean that this year's "new improved" product is anything more than a tarted-up version of last year's, or that one brand is substantially different from another.

The super-society of the Western world, with all its scientific and technical wonders, is yet more coercive than any previous incarnation, harmful incidentally not only to its overseas conquests but to its own people as well. Commercial mass culture homogenizes and levels culture at home as well as abroad; it overrides and ignores the rich diversity of American society, which, like Canada's, hosts vast regional differences, ethnic groups and subcultures. Knowing that, we should have no illusions about the designs of American culture on our country. What some French writers call *les industries de la conscience* have become the primary vehicles for the deployment of American hegemony around the world.

The word *conscience* in French has the significance here of both "conscience" and "consciousness" in English. In either language, we are talking about the influence of the mass distribution of American books, music and movies (the output of the cultural industries), though we should not forget the work of IBM, McDonald's, General Motors and their like in America's modern-day army of occupation. What are Kentucky Fried Chicken and the Big Mac if not American know-how made with local ingredients; the franchise is the retail trade's version of the branch plant.

Our intention is not to criticize the content of mass communications and information systems from the standpoint of another culture, ours or anyone else's, but to try to reveal the underlying conventions justifying the present imbalance, which is leading to the destruction of local cultures everywhere.

The consciousness industries, we now realize, are not the small-time cottage operations they once were. Since World War II and particularly in the past few years, they have assumed the size and economic proportions of heavy industry. In Canada alone, their combined worth by 1980 was almost $6 billion a year—bigger than pulp and paper or steel, as the prime minister himself noted. Moreover, they follow the same practices as other private businesses, using similar methods to the same ends. What interests us here are the dominant ideas associated with and propagated by the mass media about itself and the functioning of modern society.

It is clear that in the mass media, as in other industries, inflation has taken its toll. At every stage of the game, agents and middlemen congregate to carve off a piece of the action for themselves: producers, retailers, admen, managers and, naturally, lawyers and accountants. This keeps a lot of people busy, but it also means that a complicated bureaucracy has been superimposed on a once relatively simple exchange, leaving the original protagonists—the artist who created the work and the audience who enjoy it—relatively powerless over the conduct of the whole affair. The methods of industrialization being standardization and centralization, we can see the tremendous implications when the products involved are books and not bottle caps.

Where the consciousness industries are concerned, standardization and centralization are also used to legitimize the system itself, to disguise the actual supports of national and international powers. Mass culture, as many people have said, offers a diversion from real life. But along with élite culture, it presents a picture of the world that assumes more or less the *status quo*.

Since economics, politics and culture cannot be isolated from one another, we should also examine their relationship to science and technology, which are said to be founded on the twin principles of objectivity and neutrality. We should, in short, consider science and technology as an ideology.

There are people who deplore the way technology is used by ruling classes and states as instruments of social control, but who naïvely believe the solution is as simple as replacing the bosses with new bosses and instituting more human values. This is the case, for example, with the German essayist and poet Hans Magnus Enzensberger, who first coined the term "industries of consciousness." In denouncing their abuse by the powerful, Enzensberger nonetheless believed in the impassivity of the hardware transmitting the messages. According to the same wisdom, the natural and social sciences are objective when carried out in the antiseptic environment of the lab, according to the rules of scientific procedure. Nothing could be less probable. No research takes place in a void. There is choice and judgment involved in the selection of the subjects to be studied, both by the researchers and by the universities, governments and private foundations that fund their work. Science, to the extent that it is a collective undertaking, reflects the values and interests of the people and institutions conducting it.

Knowledge is power. And in our society, the ideals of universality and objectivity are sacred mottos to the power élite. For with these terms, they are able to pass off domination and suppression as part of the natural order of things, however detestable or unfortunate.

Of course the powerful are not the only ones who believe it. That such absolutes exist and are actually realizable is basic dogma in Western ideology. Our inherited intellectual tradition has made a fetish of masking its own prejudices by attributing them to all mankind and, where possible, to the cosmos as well. Not so long ago, serious American academics were confidently announcing the end of all ideology — Daniel Bell at Columbia University wrote an entire book on the subject — failing utterly to appreciate how transparent and hypocritical this would seem to others — the Vietnamese, for instance.

It isn't only demagogues and sociologists, however, who

perpetuate the myth. The so-called scientific community is as guilty as any of living complacently within an invisible ideology. As two scientists, J.M. Lévy-Leblond and A. Joubert, pointed out in a recent book entitled *(Auto) critique de la science* ("A Self-Criticism of Science"), by leaving the old assumptions unchallenged:

> the intellectual tacitly accepts and submits to the confusion reigning between *operative objectivity . . .* or the rules of good experimentation, and *theoretical objectivity*. The latter presupposes that a synthetic knowledge can be acquired that covers the real world (that is, the totality of mankind's historical experience) and that in due course will secure control of the universe. (our translation)

If scientists can be so deluded, how about the rest of us? To the lay person, scientists and experts are the repository of objective knowledge; their job is to give technical and socially unbiased advice. These experts, and their fields of expertise, grow in number day by day. (Childbirth became the preserve of experts when the male medical profession took over from midwives and then had them declared illegal.) Wherever they appear, these experts feign disinterest, presenting their world as the product of practical common sense and scientific testing. But behind the lauded principles of pure and ahistorical universality lurk the operative interests of class and state. The Italian physicist Marcello Cini writes in the same volume:

> We are led to contest the dogma of scientific neutrality . . . insofar as we have become aware that it is no longer possible to separate the object of our research from the reasons for choosing it, to distinguish between the reality being studied and its formulation by society, to isolate the process of finding solutions from the mechanisms that pose the problems in the first place; in other words, we have become conscious that reality is not virgin nature . . . but a product of human history, . . . which has led people to establish definite social ties among themselves.

As long as scientific research is almost purely speculative, a matter of theory, it can easily pretend to neutrality and objectivity; but the moment it is applied, it becomes part of the apportioning of power and the exercise of social control. Of particular interest to us here are the means of mass communication—the hardware it uses, the logic it follows and the ideological environment in which it operates.

Hardware is the most difficult aspect to study because it seems, in principle at any rate, to be equally accessible to whoever might wish to use it. While we can easily see that the information it carries is charged with values and judgments, it is not so easy to recognize that the carrier itself is also value-laden. We are referring here to the fact that a technology, such as the telephone, is made up of a series of components— lines, transmitters, switching stations as well as the apparatus hanging on the wall—and that each involves an intricate series of decisions about what the combined product ought to be able to do. Anyone who truly thinks all telephones are alike ought to try using one in England, where that awkward business of pushing a coin release after the call is answered seems designed to discourage its use.

The point is that the choice of hardware affects the use that can or will be made of it, and as we have found out, once adopted and installed, the hardware has a way of shaping everything that passes through it. So it is that mass-produced motor cars operate on gasoline, although we are quite capable of making engines that run on other fuels—say, renewable ones.

We can agree that industrial techniques were not developed by chance, that they have been designed and organized by particular societies to serve chosen purposes. This is what David Dickson had in mind in his study *Alternative Technology*, when he defined technology as "an abstract concept embracing both the tools and the machines used by a society, and the relations between them implied by their use . . . . [This] definition allows us to see technology in common with the legal or educational system, as social institutions."

As the post-industrial age matured in the Sixties, writers in many countries picked up on the theme of technology's hidden meaning. In France, Castoriadis wrote in *Encyclopaedia Universalis*:

> Technique seems to be value-free, neutral in value, referring to efficiency as its single quality. Yet on the scale of history such assumptions are fallacious. The idea that we are free to use this or that

instrument or process in isolation completely disappears when put in the context of the entire set of techniques "possessed" by a society or an age but which, by the same token, "possesses" it. (our translation)

He added, "Every society creates its own internal and external world, and from this creation, technique is neither an instrument nor a cause but a dimension—because it is present wherever society constructs what for it is the real and the rational."

A great part of our thinking about technology and society in recent times has been taken up in the debate over whether its role is as a determinant or a symptom of social change. Through various interpretations these two positions generally hold, on the one hand, that technology, discovered by independent scientific research, conditions and creates new ways of life; and on the other hand, that technology is a by-product, but one element in the process of change already in progress and one that is produced by other circumstances. In both views, technology is treated as if it were self-defining and self-creating, evolving according to its own internal, purely scientific logic.

No one writer has epitomized this fallacy better than Marshall McLuhan, despite the fact that he became famous for his theories about the nature and the distinguishing features of various media—speech, print, radio and television. But to cite Raymond Williams again, McLuhan never understood these media as "social practices." What interested him about television was the physical and emotional experience of watching a TV set; its main significance for him lay in its relation to the individual as an extension of human sensory faculties. So the medium is the message, not the program it transmits; and the viewer, in McLuhan parlance, becomes the content of whatever he or she is watching. The Italian viewing *Loveboat* is not watching American television at all, but Italian television!

Despite his reputation as an iconoclast, McLuhan was in the end merely offering a trendy functionalist elaboration of the old formalist analysis, which had already heavily influenced the study of literature and language as well as psychology and sociology in the United States. He produced a theory of the mass media that matched conventional political ideology and was at the same time compatible with the prevailing styles and theories. It also perfectly matched the "international" style of American avant-garde painting of the Fifties, Sixties and Seventies, which still stands as the most graphic demonstration of the triumph of form over content. Call it abstract expressionism, colour-field painting or minimalism, the meaning of the work is stripped down to the arrangement of paint on canvas.

It must be true, then, that a technology loses its meaning outside the social and economic system it belongs to; clearly one cannot have capitalist economics without capitalist technique, and vice versa. Just as we can show how the powers that be in socialist countries patronize "socialist realist" art, so we can interpret the art patronized by élites in the West as "capitalist realist" art and see in like manner how it is a fitting symbol for its own reigning ideology. Technological institutions are deeply enmeshed in the life and ideals of the society that produces and uses them. If this is difficult to verify in practical terms, it may be because we think of mass culture as merchandise to be consumed, exported, used up. And as Marx has said, merchandise hides the interaction of production and exploitation, of domination and alienation.

At first glance, nothing could seem less ideological than a television set. It is merely an artifact that groups or individuals can use as they will. If there are criticisms to be levelled, it is for the unimaginative use made of it by those who own and program the networks.

Back in 1932, the great German playwright and philosopher Bertolt Brecht expressed the hope that radio would become a genuine medium of communication instead of the apparatus of distribution it then was. Forty years later Enzensberger took up Brecht's theme in *The Consciousness Industry*, when he wrote, "Monopolistic capitalism develops the consciousness-shaping industry more quickly and more extensively than other sectors of production; it must at the same time fetter it. A socialist media theory has to work at this contradiction."

Like Brecht, Enzensberger criticizes the way the media function without questioning the implications of the communications technology itself. Yet, when we examine what has been wrought, all we have actually achieved with these sophisticated communications is a distortion of *communication*. Communication is quite explicitly excluded from the mass media. To quote French socialist Jean Baudrillard, in *Pour une critique de l'économie politique de signe* ("A Critique of the Political Economy of Signs"):

> What characterizes the mass media is the fact that they are anti-mediators and intransitive; that they are in the business of non-communication — if one accepts the definition of communication as an *exchange*, where word and *response* are reciprocated, where there is, in short, *responsibility* — and not a psychological or moral responsibility but a personal correlation between one individual and another within the exchange. Put another way, communication ought to be defined as something more than this simple one-way transmission of a message, even if this message is reacted to in the "feedback." The architecture of media is founded on the ultimate definition, that *they banish any reply forever*; they make response impossible (except in some *artificial* form that is itself integrated into the process of emission and that in no way alters the unilaterality of communication). This is their real abstraction. And it is on this abstraction that the system of power and social control is based. (our translation)

The form of communication we have accepted imposes its own technological environment and with it a cultural format that allows neither alternatives nor the opportunity to answer back. In this way, communications have become an extension of bureaucracies that are themselves non-reciprocal, unresponsive and often irresponsible as well.

What one could point out to Baudrillard is that his own television set is an instrument of social control sitting right in his living room, one that promises to keep people from talking to one another, isolated in a darkened room in front of a glowing box. The same thing could be happening in education and in industry, where many jobs can be performed without any human or social contact. When people no longer have to see or talk to each other, a small group holding power will be able to make decisions for all of us without fear of reprisal or rebellion from the citizenry. A bona fide 1984 scenario arriving right on time!

By acknowledging the unilaterality of the media, we uncover the linking of economics and politics, with their technical forms acting together with global coherence. This unilaterality, we must understand, is implied in the technology that presupposes passive consumption, but it is also related to the fact that access to the creative, the input side of the operation, is strictly controlled. Whether we consider news agencies (wire services), book publishing or data banks, the responsibility for programming the mass media, for producing and selecting the content, rests in the hands of an ominously small number of people whose influence is augmented by the fact that ownership of the media is also concentrated among a very small number of very large corporations. It is this imbalance between sender and receiver that prompted someone to remark that freedom of the press really belongs to those who own the presses. So, too, with television and telecommunications.

Today mind-boggling advances in the technology of information storage and delivery (microchip computers, fibre optics and video cassettes) have turned computer communications into a major growth industry within the span of a decade. But the data banks now being amassed are, for the most part, leased commercially, which means that their content is almost exclusively made up of financial and technical information. These data systems criss-crossing the world via satellites are the invisible threads holding the transnational corporate empires together.

We need hardly remind anyone that ours is the age of information. Where transportation was once the key to economic prowess and supremacy, today it is telecommunications; where food supply used to be the lifeline keeping the armies of the empire marching, now satellite communication is the strategic support for US and Soviet military manoeuvres around the world. It is not surprising, as more and more communication is done by satellite — while advance weapons wizards have been perfecting techniques for conducting photo-reconnaisance from space, with resolution power enough to distinguish a Ford from a Chevy at an altitude of 150 miles — to hear about the hunter-killer satellites that, as the name suggests, track down and blow up the other side's "spies in the sky." Canada, which was a pioneer in the domestic use of satellite communication, has more recently contributed the Canadarm to the US extraterrestrial military effort. Aside from opening up the possibility of holding World War III in space, satellites are revolutionizing conventional communications, including radio and television.

In Canada, cable television began its terrestrial conquest in the late Sixties, when an ambitious gang of cable companies were licensed to deliver television to Canadian households. By 1981, close to fifty-five per cent of the country was hooked up, making this the most cabled nation in the world.

Unlike the telephone, cable TV carries signals in one

direction only, though the day is fast arriving (and field tests are under way) when it will be replaced by two-way cable (possibly made of optical fibres that transmit signals by laser beams along hair-thin glass wires), making the television set "interactive" and opening up a whole new horizon for home information systems. It will enable consumers to buy real estate, read the newspapers, pay the bills, access data banks and send letters without leaving their living-room terminals.

Meanwhile, science continues to find new ways of combining information modes and systems (digital, audio, video) that used to be separate. The computer can be linked to the telephone, creating what has been named telematics, and in a twinkling of the eye your television set becomes the display unit for a word processor or videotex system. The computer is now a mass medium, available at department stores everywhere, in pocket calculators and video games. Behind the scenes in the communications industry, the big struggle that underlies all other debates — about cable services, satellite broadcasting and so on — is over who will control that two-way wire running into our homes and offices: the telephone company, the cable companies, private industry or public enterprise? Obviously there is a lot more than just money involved in the concept of the "wired world" of tomorrow.

Meanwhile, what will happen to privacy, to cultural diversity, to democracy when instant opinion polls and referendums are possible? Even now, there are data systems in operation that monitor our lives in a way that would have been unthinkable to all but science fiction writers a few decades ago. There are computers somewhere keeping tabs on every long-distance telephone call we make, recording all our bank transactions and our use of health insurance. Moreover, there are people tending these computers who have access to personal information about our credit, our health and our police records that even we don't have. These computers know more about ourselves than we do, and certainly far more than any centralized brains trust, human or electronic, *ought* to know.

One thing is certain: communications technology is bound to increase exponentially the power of organizations like IBM and AT&T, the Exxons of the future. For if energy supply is essential to the smooth running of the economy, so too is information.

In recent years the cultural industries have been caught up by the merger fervour sweeping American business, and many of the largest firms have been corralled into conglomerates like

Gulf and Western, RCA or American Express that may publish books out of one division while running a railroad or manufacturing pantyhose from another. This structural change not only concentrates ownership, further reducing the number of directors and decision-makers and increasing their individual power; it also diversifies that power across vast and varied networks of interlocking interests.

For example, RCA, the well-known leader in electronic and aerospace engineering, is also the parent company of NBC and six publishing firms, including Random House and Alfred A. Knopf. Under its aegis are also to be found RCA Records, Hertz Auto Rentals, Banquet Foods and a host of other companies dealing in real estate, furnishings, cable TV and radio; it owns the Alaska long-line telephone system and the Satcom communications satellites. It operates in all the key media and on all sides of the industry and, to put it mildly, has an influence far greater than the sum of its parts. IBM, which invents, patents and manufactures information machinery for the world market, has its own satellite network in operation, offering data service to industrial and commercial clients; it has recently announced plans to enter the programming market with video discs. The hardware giants are getting into software and tightening the circle.

Moreover, over the last few years, the consciousness industries have developed a new international marketing strategy, based on the idea of cross-media promotion, which parallels the integration taking place in their financial structure. It consists of taking one idea, like *Star Wars* or *E.T.*, and running it through a chain of production in as many media as possible: with the movie come the sound-track recording, the official book, a TV series, comic strip and so on. The theme is affixed to as many saleable objects as possible—lunch pails, T-shirts, posters and puzzles—and translated into computer games or a new line of men's fashions.

The results have been dramatic. EMI Records, a British firm that produced the Beatles and is now a subsidiary of Paramount Pictures, sold fifteen million copies of *Saturday Night Fever* in less than one year in the United States, half again as many as any one of the Beatles' albums ever sold in the US.

While the change is not obviously visible from the consumer's viewpoint, the impact of this speeded-up commercialism on the creative side of the business has been immediate and devastating. In Europe and the United States, as well as in Canada, there is serious talk about the demise of serious literature. For when driven by the commercial imperative, any industry will naturally seek to reduce the risks, or to build in a success factor. In the old days, Hollywood had the star system; then came formula sitcoms and spin-offs with television. Now we are treated to the spectacle of a single style, such as urban cowboy or punk, mounted as a vast promotional campaign to sell everything and anything that can sport a logo. A great deal of corporate effort and inventiveness today is spent on packaging the super-bestseller that will capture astronomic sales and the rapt attention of the world for fifteen minutes.

This new thrust by the largest companies sets off a ripple effect through the industry, as the souped-up superculture encroaches on the markets of smaller, local and often nationally or independently owned segments of the industry. In order to stay afloat, the latter are compelled to follow suit by opting for crowd-pleasers, too, while cutting back on their own marginal output—which could mean the experimental, the new or simply the little-known. The industry as a whole loses diversity and originality as the conglomerates pre-empt creativity.

Of course cultural conglomerates are administered in the same fashion as any other industrial entity; and even their concept of freedom of information will be strategically subordinated, in the final analysis, to the corporate goals of accumulating capital. Illustrating the kind of economic weight the cultural industries pull in the American economy, the US Department of Commerce estimated that fifty per cent of the GNP in 1978 was tied to "information transfers," up from forty per cent in 1970, when fifty-three per cent of salary payments and forty per cent of the work-force were accounted for by information-related industries. In 1980, AT&T broke all records when it reported an after-tax profit of $6 billion.

Information is good business, obviously; but more to the point, the vast transnational enterprise of the United States depends on there being no barriers to its unimpeded flow. American communications critic Herbert Schiller has explored this symbiosis and the methods by which, as he puts it, the $2-trillion US economy is maintained at home and extended beyond its borders.

Ideologically, he detects three basic, non-negotiable beliefs at work, the first and most important being the concept of the free flow of information. Clearly, here is a reciprocity between cultural domination and economic imperialism, for inasmuch as American capitalism requires the free flow of goods and capital, so, too, in its cultural guise, does it depend on the free flow of information; as Schiller remarks in *Who Knows*, "Freedom of information is treated as an extension of the charter of the International Trade Organization."

In Western democracies, everybody is sensitive to the need to be well informed. Whoever dares question such freedom is quickly labelled a Stalin or a Khomeini. Nevertheless, we must at least look at what this involves and judge for ourselves whether freedom or licence is being exercised. Can complete freedom ever exist in a flow that is, by its own design, crammed full of interpreters and selectors? The idea that it can conceals more than it reveals, for it glosses over the fact that some people—for example, broadcasters—are more free than others to communicate.

According to Schiller, the second article of faith holds that if communications are organized in any other way than along the lines of private enterprise, there is a danger that some degree of unfreedom will occur. Freedom of information in the United States is closely identified with private ownership of communications.

The third element in the triad is the convention that corporations, in more than just a legalistic sense, have human rights. In other words, they are assumed to have the same rights under the law as those guaranteed to individuals by the Bill of Rights. The peculiar astigmatism of American ideology is that it applies freedom, as in "freedom of speech," equally to corporations and to individuals; but corporations can much more easily afford to indulge their freedom with scant regard for the rights of individuals and minorities who lack an equal means to reply.

Schiller explains that there are some beliefs specific to communications, chiefly the maxim that information is a commodity. This may sound like a practical way of looking at things, but it turns attention toward the economic transaction and away from the social and public relationship involved. There is also great popular confusion between abundance and diversity. Multiplicity of outlets (stores in a chain, stations in a network) does not necessarily multiply choice—quite the opposite. Mass marketing promotes, as we have remarked before, uniformity, duplication and repetition. A third hallowed belief uncritically accepted is that the interdependence of the nations of the modern world takes priority over local interests. While this invokes a cosy, "we're all in this together" sentiment, it also tends to sanctify existing arrangements and inequalities and sanctions the suppression of reform.

One would naturally expect the transnationals to be unsympathetic to economic protectionism or to any nationalist policy that might lead to the erection of obstacles in the path of moving goods or capital. Sooner or later conflict can be expected between the multinational and the objective of one or another host country. However, putting quotas on the importation of textiles or small foreign cars is one thing; the country that proposes regulating the flow of information, even in the interests of protecting national sovereignty, will be accused of censorship, even of violating human rights.

With information so important to our society and the strongest influence in the environment, the possibility of multinationals forming *de facto* world governments is fast becoming a probability. Boardroom-to-boardroom diplomacy and regulation of markets by private business deals already constitute economic policy without representation. Transnationals make agreements affecting international relations without ever troubling to go through political channels.

This is what Zbigniew Brzezinski describes in his book *Between Two Ages: America's Role in the Technetronic Era*, where he suggests the world is heading toward more streamlined supranational structures. Maintaining that the United States is the first "global society" in history and extolling the new global consciousness developing among the intellectual élites, he points out that "a rudimentary framework of global social and economic institutions has already taken shape." He cites world organizations like the United Nations, the International Monetary Fund, the World Bank and the OECD, mechanisms for integrating and co-ordinating world trade in which the US has played the integrator among integrators. But rather than proposing a world government based on nation-states, he promotes the idea of a community of developed nations (initially comprising Western Europe, Japan and the US) as a way of increasing "the possibility of a long-range strategy for international development . . . [and] paving the way for more internationalized, multilateral foreign aid." Brzezinski concludes, "Such an approach would also tend to end the debate over American globalism." And yet, "The fact is that much of the initiative and impetus for an undertaking on so grand a scale will have to come from the United States."

The technetronic era, we discover, is a euphemism for American empire; one in which the boundaries between nations as well as between private and public enterprise are blurred, in which a new global unity replaces the old isolated and divided structures of "established cultures, deeply entrenched religions and distinctive national identities."

In reality, the global city, as Brzezinski calls it, already exists. In the world of private enterprise, the multinationals, led by the corporate giants with assets and annual budgets larger than those of most countries, established their networks long ago; these include the food and drug companies that sell powdered milk to Third World mothers and Valium to middle-class women in the West, and the consciousness industries, proselytizing American consumerism from Istanbul to Inuvik and, of course, the technology that Brzezinski would have us believe is pressing a new world upon us.

Alongside the political power structure run commercial and economic ones, and the interdependence between the two goes far beyond mere corporate contributions to political party coffers. Their destinies are intertwined. As the American historian Joseph Tolchin has noted, with the coming of the American imperial age, the private sector became an agent of the United States — that is, of the state itself. Never more than under Ronald Reagan, the tight alliance between government and business is the basis of US politics. There is no doubt that the multinationals are central to the American enterprise and are considered a stabilizing and unifying influence in the world, a kind of global civilizing force. Not only must the world be made safe for American capitalism, America and American culture must be promoted abroad. Thus spake Henry Luce, publisher of *Time* and *Life* magazines. Sensing the opportunity the US would have after World War II, he urged Americans "to accept wholeheartedly our duty and our opportunity as the most powerful and vital nation in the world and in consequence to exert upon the world the full impact of our influence, for such purposes as we see fit and by such means as we see fit." To which he added, "It now becomes our time to be the powerhouse from which the ideals spread throughout the world."

After 1945, the conditions of Marshall Plan aid often including permitting the distribution of American magazines (like *Time*) and American movies. At the time, Hollywood badly needed foreign markets to fill the widening gulf between expenditures and revenues lost during the war. The Motion Picture Export Association was licensed as a cartel to promote the sale of American pictures around the world. As Thomas

Guback recounts in *The International Film Industry*, Hollywood, through the MPEA (which operates its own mini-State Department abroad), then proceeded to build up its foreign markets with ingenuity and dogged determination. Today, about half of the major studios' business is abroad, Canada being their number one customer.

Canadians have had several opportunities to view the US culture lobby in action over the years. There was the infamous Canadian Co-operation Project in the Fifties, when C.D. Howe and Lester Pearson, with the help of a little Hollywood-style persuasion, traded off a nascent Canadian film production industry for a few mentions of Canada in American movies and the vague promise that this would boost tourism (in fact, tourism declined). More recently, when Parliament passed the *Time-Reader's Digest* bill in 1976, it met a tumultuous opposition inside and outside the House, complete with a publicity campaign staged by the American border stations and plenty of heavy-duty, high-level lobbying in Ottawa and Washington. At stake for the Americans were $20 million in Canadian television ad revenues.

Bill C-58 was actually an amendment to the Income Tax Act that disallowed the deduction of advertising expenses paid to non-Canadian corporations (such as the border television stations) and cancelled the special exemption given *Time* and *Reader's Digest* in the 1965 tax act. What it meant for us was an economic base for a fledgling magazine publishing industry. It had been known for some fifteen years, since the report of the O'Leary Commission on publications in 1960, that as long as half the share of advertising revenues in Canada was diverted into the two big US magazines operating here with Canadian editions, the indigenous periodical press would remain poor and underdeveloped.

Later it was learned that the US State Department and President Kennedy had interceded on behalf of *Time* when O'Leary's recommendations were finally being considered. The Auto Pact was also pending, and Washington simply made it clear that the exemption of both *Time* and *Reader's Digest* was a precondition to such an agreement. Pearson fell into line, and the following year *Time* and *Digest* raked in sixty per cent of the advertising revenues in Canada.

When Bill C-58 was enacted, *Time* (Canada) ceased publication. After complying with the new ownership regulations, *Digest* continued publishing its Canadian editions in French and English and was allowed to keep its Canadian status. (Late in 1982 this picture changed when the US parent bought the Canadian shares of its subsidiary. Although *Digest* is now a wholly foreign-owned publication, the government has yet to cancel its special postal rates.)

Meanwhile the fortunes of Canadian publishing have taken a sharp turn for the better. In five years, ad revenues doubled to $100,000 and the number of Canadian magazines increased by twenty-five percent. We now have a weekly newsmagazine of our own (*Maclean's*) that outsells *Time* (640,000 to 325,000) and several specialty magazines doing extremely well, such as *Atlantic Insight, Canadian Geographic* and *Saturday Night*, their success built on large circulations of 70,000, 100,000 and 130,000 respectively. For smaller magazines, the financial road is still rough, and the need for arts council grants hasn't diminished. They have not benefited visibly from the overall growth of the industry through these years. C-58 did ensure that the larger Canadian magazines could finally establish a presence in the marketplace, and as such it was a good example of simple yet effective legislation. It is an equally excellent illustration of American tenacity, for today Congress is still contemplating retaliatory measures.

V

Many of the arguments advanced against Canada's economic dependence on the United States, while deploring deindustrialization, nevertheless leave the impression that our chief disadvantage is in being prevented from "managing things for ourselves." The antidote for our weak condition in manufacturing and trade would seem to be a simple matter of repatriating control and ownership of business and industry. Our slide from a branch-plant to a warehouse economy will be miraculously halted, and we can go on as before, only under our own steam. Yet the real issue — and it is a challenge more than a problem — will be to do things differently. How can we deplore the effects of the empire and stop short of criticizing the goals that make it what it is? How can we go on ignoring the evidence that any restructuring of the economy means a restructuring of the value system implied by it?

According to a long essay by Armand and Michèle Mattelart in a 1979 issue of *Le Monde diplomatique*, cultural imperialism consists of "producing ideas and desires that will secure economic domination [our translation]." Just as American capitalism relies on culture to palliate the crises and support its economic hegemony, it may be that to escape from our economic straitjacket we will have to examine the cultural dimension of economic domination and figure out what cultural circumstances would permit us to escape the empire. But before broaching this task, we should stop to take note of the people who profit from the present order and how they are able to manage whatever crisis we might provoke in the *status quo*.

To begin with, there are some myths to explode. The first, already dealt with, is the assumption that technology is neutral and that our civilization can be saved by turning over the technological reins to the good guys. The second has to do with the credence our society invests in "objectivity." Scientism, as more than one theologian has mourned, is the secular religion of our time; it promises that wherever the principles of scientific inquiry are observed, objectivity will result—in research, in journalism, even in art. Science is expected to solve most of our problems: cure cancer, treat pollution, prevent war and create life when sex alone doesn't work. Understandably, the precepts, terminology and techniques used by science have seeped into other disciplines. Where philosophy was once the ultimate authority on human conduct, today the behavioural sciences have the last word.

The third myth is the one that treats certain ideals as if they were universal absolutes and uses them to rationalize the power of class and empire. For several centuries, universality has been understood as the central attribute of progress. In its vision of reality, backward classes and backwater nations naturally seek to ally themselves with others who are wealthier, more powerful—in short, more advanced. The actions of authorities, from the most restrained to the physically and symbolically most violent, are typically undertaken in the name of some sort of abstract—justice, liberty, socialism, Christian civilization or Italian futurism. And those who disagree run the risk of being treated as obscurantists, spoil-sports or, more likely, subversives.

Nothing will be spared to discredit those who cast doubt on the arbitrary structures controlling and channelling social development. In the case of Ian Adams, author of a spy novel about a fictitious RCMP secret service agent who was "turned," first by the Russians and then by the CIA, without the RCMP's knowledge, the attempt was fairly blatant. For three years, *S: Portrait of a Spy* was withdrawn from sale by Gage Publishing while Adams fought off a libel suit brought by a retired RCMP counter-espionage director who claimed "S" was a depiction of him. Not only was this the first time in Canada that a novelist was sued for libel, it was also the first time a novelist was actually directed by a judge to reveal his sources. The case was eventually settled out of court, but it nevertheless illuminates the attitude, so ingrained in our authority structures, that abhors *any* public scrutiny of their internal activity and makes a professional ethic of secrecy.

In some societies, the social order is sanctified or written into a religious code; in others it is naturalized, or written into the laws of nature. So we are told it is "human nature" when the so-called classless society of the Soviet Union turns out to be riddled with bureaucratic and party élites. The twentieth century, though no less violent than any other, invented the consciousness industries: how better to manage the world than by persuading subject peoples to accept their own suppression as a benevolence, to hail their own economic exploitation as the premium for a higher standard of living. In other epochs, tyrants like Napoleon had to raise armies and kill thousands of people to impress the French Revolution on the rest of Europe. Today the two great powers of socialism and advanced capitalism fight it out for supremacy through the developing nations of the earth, who, in doing business with one giant or the other, adopt the appropriate social model as an ideal, so reinforcing the process of universalization.

Neutrality, objectivity and universality: these are the three precepts on which the American empire runs. Related to and supporting them are two others: the right to the free flow of information and the pursuit of excellence—that vague but piously intoned *raison d'être* of élite culture.

As the consumer society is coming under fire from consumers themselves, we hear from the likes of Brzezinski and Bernard Ostry that Western civilization is approaching its apogee, when science will make it possible for everyone to be a part of (if not a participant in) the information society. Meanwhile, society remains continually in need of material goods and ever-larger quantities of symbolic goods. When mercantilism was the order of the day, the state that possessed the most powerful means of transporting raw materials took the lead. Later the advantage passed to those who manufactured superior products. Today, the laurels belong to those who can control symbolic goods. The new multinational conglomerates have taken the rule of vertical integration, so effective in the oil industry, and applied it to the information industry. Here, too, they can invariably be found working both sides of the street, providing or controlling both hardware and software; that is, both the distribution systems and the programming carried by them. It is not surprising that the country producing the majority of the world's traffic in television programs (UNESCO estimates seventy per cent) also exports the equipment and eagerly offers its expertise to help set up TV networks in the developing nations. All three of the American commercial television networks have been involved in designing, constructing and programming for systems abroad: in Africa, the Middle East, Europe and Central America, and in 1976, NBC got the contract to build a national TV system for South Vietnam.

Life in the United States becomes everybody's paragon of good thinking and right doing. Very quickly small nations, hungry for American culture to fill their mini-American cultural systems, fall into the trap of forsaking their own creativity for imitation, and local élites, having the closest associations with American culture, help to prejudice the situation by importing imperial standards and tastes into the colony. The force of American consumerism can convince whole populations that excellence means American. For the colonials, this means that it is fashionable and often expedient to turn one's back on one's own country, because positing one's own cultural reference means rejecting excellence itself.

The habit has proven to be tragically difficult to break, and not only for countries like Nicaragua and El Salvador. More democratic places like Jamaica and Canada have found it equally hard to get off the merry-go-round, or even, at times, to see the necessity for doing so. On reflection it does seem curious that Canada, which has been ingesting massive doses of US influence far longer than anyone else, has not been front and centre among the opponents of America's communications revolution. Instead the impetus has come from underdeveloped nations.

The Third World has used UNESCO as its main forum for protesting the *status quo* in world communications. There, it has been pointed out that the circulation of news and entertainment programs and the purchase of communications equipment are the results of international commercial activity that benefits a few technologically and industrially advanced nations. The flow of global communications, while "free" for these nations, is imbalanced and one-sided and tends to flow from the rich and powerful to the poor and weak. Some countries are actually in the position of having to rely on foreign news agencies not only to convey their news to the world, but to transmit news to their own citizens as well. The situation tends to preserve old colonial patterns, making the problem of underdevelopment all the more perplexing.

One UNESCO document, *Aims and Approaches to a New International Communications Order*, puts it this way:

> The values and ideas of a consumer civilization which are transmitted from rich countries through the mass media, often conflict with the fundamental interests and values of other countries. It is not only that they strike at traditional forms of cultural life and identity, but they provoke even deeper conflicts between poverty and wealth, between wishes and possibilities, and lead to increasingly sharper differentiation between the masses and the small elite which adopts the ways of thought and of life offered through television and films and other foreign models.

Several years ago now, Jacques Berque published his seminal study of the colonization of North Africa by the French, *La Dépossession du monde* (*The Dispossession of the World*), in which he stated that the last phase of colonialism— following the dispossession of natural resources, the land and the economy— is the dispossession of the people themselves, which is to say, their self-image, memory and collective traditions. As the image of the colonizer invades their identity, it imposes another heritage and history, binding the colony to another vision of the future. So the wheel turns. Self-deprecation and an insipid masochism ensue, accelerating the corrosion of the indigenous culture, while the other natural resources are also being depleted.

If information is understood to include all manner of data and imagery, it is clear that no production requiring large sums of money can be free. Not all of us have the same access to the airwaves or the pages of the morning newspaper. Nor, as we've said, are information systems free in the sense that we all have the right to decide what programming will be provided. Our freedom resides almost exclusively in the right to consume (or not to consume) what others have decided to put before us. For those in charge, the trick is to manipulate public demand in order to reduce the risk, which explains why the natural instinct of any commercial system is toward the creation of a monopoly—the ultimate in marketing. Far from bringing more participants or greater free play into the exchange, free passage of information has actually been used as a private right by American corporations to monopolize the exchange.

Nor is there anything like absolute freedom for those who write the messages. No message is completely free of values or ideology, and there is great deception in thinking that messages, productions and creations, whether in élite or mass culture systems, emanate freely from the minds of free individuals who are at complete liberty to say or express whatever they think or feel.

Aware of the complex issues surrounding communications, many governments have made policy in the communications field a priority. In an effort to determine the effect of US pre-eminence on information and culture in its broadest sense, the president of France commissioned an inquiry into the implications of the information society in 1978. In their report, *L'Informatisation de la société* ("The Informationalized Society"), the authors took the position that a national telecommunications policy is a blueprint of the nervous system of the body politic and should be regarded above all as a plan for social change. About American influence, the report stated: "[This] vigilance is indicative of the will to check American domination which is even stronger here [in the field of telecommunications] than in other areas . . . and this at a time when world conflicts are predominantly cultural and when the appropriation of culture has become a motive force of history [our translation]."

Brzezinski writes:

> It is American society that is currently having the greatest impact on all other societies, prompting a far-reaching cumulative transformation in their outlook and mores . . . .
>
> This is all the more likely because American society, more than any other, "communicates" with the entire globe. Roughly sixty-five per cent of all world communications originate in this country. Moreover, the United States has been most active in the promotion of a global communications system by means of satellites, and it is pioneering the development of a world-wide information grid . . . . For the first time in history the cumulative knowledge of mankind will be made accessible on a global scale—and it will be almost instantaneously available in response to demand.

If sixty-five per cent of the world's communications do indeed emanate from the United States, are we to assume — can we logically assume — that American messages diffused so efficiently by American hardware are in the best interests and to the general advantage of all humanity?

VI

Until recently one of the fundamental assumptions of free enterprise has been that nature is man's to exploit. As a result, industry has destroyed fragile ecosystems and may well have irretrievably polluted the planet. Everyone knows this and yet transnational capitalism, headquartered in certain countries and among certain classes, still seems to be on the ascendant. The imbalances persist, and everywhere we hear talk about the rise of the new conservatism; not the old conservativism of conservation, but the kind that champions more and freer free enterprise — the freedom to go on wasting nature. Among nations and people, the rich get richer, and the poor tighten their cardboard belts. Once again large resources are being thrown into an effort to insulate the American economy and its technological apparatus from the challenging times, to perpetuate its hierarchy and its inequality.

Meanwhile governments are finding it harder than ever to keep the economy growing. Very plainly the pie has stopped expanding, and capitalism is faced with a problem of apocalyptic proportions, because economic growth is the *only* way it knows how to satisfy demands made on the system for equality and fairer treatment. What keeps its victims from rebelling is social security, but that won't solve the problem.

To put it bluntly, the crisis is not some passing thing. And it has been upon us for quite some time. The Sixties and Seventies raised a great many issues that cut deep into liberal democracy's reputation for fair play and justice. Every part of everyone's everyday life was put up for re-evaluation: work, education, the family, relations between the sexes, attitudes toward minorities, children, women, the nation and other societies. The problem is very deep-seated and emphatically cultural, for the turbulence is affecting our most fundamental social habits and customs. It has been given many names: the decline of the West, the end of humanism, the coming of post-industrial society, the scientific-technological revolution. That such a change-over is occurring in our society seems now to be generally understood, although there is no consensus about where it is taking us. The technologists, futurists and pollsters make their predictions, but they are turning out to be no more enlightened than the rest of us. For many, the future looks grim. Professor George C. Lodge, a member of that respected Bostonian family and hardly a subversive, has written, "The United States is in the throes of a huge transformation comparable to the one which finished off the Middle Ages, which razed institutions to pave the way for modernity."

Another well-known American conservative, Daniel Bell, has written at length about the cultural contradictions of capitalism that he sees undermining American society. Western civilization is coming to a watershed that will bring about the end of modernism, the cultural movement that Bell says has dominated the arts and symbolic expression throughout the twentieth century. Modernism has put capitalism into a double bind: economic expansion and the creation of new capital has been achieved, but by means of a new set of virtues and ethics that are, at heart, antithetical to and in conflict with the original motivations of capitalism. Modernism pits plastic credit against the Protestant ethic. One could conclude that at the very moment America is achieving the ultimate empire through cultural domination, its own culture is shipping water on all sides and threatens to sink. The old Protestant belief in hard work and deferred pleasure has given way to its extreme opposite — play now and pay later. And all of it has been at the instigation of capitalism itself.

Bell sees America as if it were fulfilling Marx's prophecy, self-destructing under the weight of its own contradictions. "American capitalism has lost its traditional legitimacy which was bred on a moral system of reward rooted in the Protestant sanctification of work. It has substituted a hedonism which promises material ease and luxury." In Bell's view, the radical disjunction of economics, politics and culture afoot in American society is bad news, the kind of situation that historically has "paved the way for more direct social revolution."

Alvin Toffler, a somewhat more middle-brow observer of the American scene, followed his bestselling *Future Shock* with *The Third Wave*, in which he, too, claims "something revolutionary is happening. We are participating not merely in the birth of a new organizational form but in the birth of a new civilization" — which is throwing the (still present) Second Wave systems into crisis. In a nutshell, Toffler's thesis is that the first great age of human development was dominated by agriculture, which after several millennia was succeeded by industrialization, which in its turn, after scarcely a century, is yielding to the third age, the age of the new electronic and cybernetic technology.

Toffler sees the root of our manifold crises in the clash between the systems and institutions inherited from the industrial age (welfare, the post office and large hospitals) and the new technologies, which imply a different method of organization — smaller-scale and decentralized. Characteristic of the Third Wave is the home computer, technological experimentation, do-it-yourself health care, home maintenance and home-made ethics, new forms of the family and new attitudes toward jobs and careers. He writes of the public resistance to technology, about the "techno-rebels" who may, without knowing it, be agents of the Third Wave.

> They begin not with technology but with hard questions about what kind of future society we want. They recognize that we have so many technological opportunities we can no longer find, develop and apply them all. They argue therefore the need to select more carefully among them, to choose those technologies that serve long-range social and economic goals. Rather than letting technology shape our goals, they wish to assert social control over the larger direction of the technological thrust.

With his keen nose for change, Toffler makes intriguing reading, and although he allows that adjustments to the Third Wave world will bring casualties, he doubts neither its imminence nor the inevitability of its arrival. Nor does he pause to evaluate the political aspects of the situation and the possibility of confrontation between the vested interests of the Second Wave and those of the Third.

There is a familiar ring of unreality here, for Toffler, too, seems to treat technology as a free and self-determining agent; he never addresses the question of, say, whether solar energy will be developed because it makes sense in the long run, or only when the oil companies find a way of harnessing the sun and running it through a meter. According to Toffler, the struggle to maintain industrial age systems is a losing battle, a squabble over deck-chairs on the *Titanic*. Obviously, to the programmers of the new information systems will go the spoils of the future, but to suggest that the future will belong to the people who today propose reform, who no longer believe the endemic problems of hunger, poverty, urban decay and crime can be treated under the present industrial order, presumes a major shift in the existing power structure. These people may be in the vanguard of Toffler's Third Wave, but that has never guaranteed anyone anything but an excellent chance of catching grape-shot.

Since the Sixties, the tensions and dangers of technology and industry experienced by ordinary people in their everyday lives have led to rebellious and deviant behaviour that has by now become a kind of norm. The ban-the-bomb and anti-war movements of the Sixties continued into the anti-nuclear and environment lobbies of the Seventies and were once again on the march in the early Eighties. Moreover, people who would never have engaged in civil disobedience a decade ago are doing it today. Workers laid off by the closings of US branch plants occupy their factories in protest; farmers outraged by the banks' foreclosing on neighbours block the roadways to prevent the removal of farm equipment for sale at auction; the women of Amqui, Quebec, occupy the local police station and with one-quarter of the town's population, hold up a Via train to force the government to alter its decision to locate a much-needed paper-mill elsewhere.

As television spreads, carrying news and public information into practically every household, the percentage of the population who bother to vote in most elections has fallen off, while participation in other kinds of political activity, especially demonstrations and strikes, has risen dramatically. That in itself is a bellwether of our times. And judging by the popularity and effect of this sort of political activism, it is no longer reasonable to assume that the effective opposition sits in the benches of Her Majesty's Loyal Opposition. Today it more likely lies in wait outside the House with bull-horns and placards. By the same token, the lunatic fringe has never been so active, fielding candidates for people who want to vote but who can't take elections seriously any more. In the 1983 British election, the Raving Loony Party ran a green chicken and the Rural Revival Party called for the reintroduction of horse-drawn transport. Canada's own Rhinoceros Party has been campaigning on puns and *non sequitur*s for fifteen years, and in some ridings in Quebec, it has actually polled more votes than the Conservatives.

This turn of events reflects a number of factors, including loss of confidence in the political process, in the integrity of politicians and bureaucrats and even in the efficacy of electoral politics. The tendency has been therefore for the disaffected to organize around discrete causes (conservation, human rights) or single issues (abortion, censorship). But this has nonetheless touched the lives of an extraordinary number of ordinary citizens. Many have become political for the first time in their lives; they have found lawyers, formed committees, elected leaders and issued press releases, all in order to short-circuit the politicians and take their case directly (via the evening news) to other citizens. This field is by no means restricted to terrorists, extremists or idealistic kids. At least a hundred thousand people, anti-nuke grannies, babies and others, took to the streets in the spring of 1983 to protest testing of the Cruise missile in Canada.

Meanwhile, reality forces itself upon us. Progress marches on and the omens are pondered in the hopes that the economy will soon recover its strength. But the Fifties and Sixties, as they recede into the past, look more and more like a historical aberration—a golden age. The machines producing material and symbolic goods are showing definite signs of fatigue. The élites responsible for setting them in motion to begin with behave as if there were no choice but to follow their inherent logic to whatever end. In the grip of disaster, they can only mutter prayers for moderation and "restraint"—that watchword of our times. Who hasn't noticed Hollywood's deepening obsession with disaster flicks and horror movies—coinciding, not so coincidentally perhaps, with the nostalgia craze for old fashions and for all the old decades, one after another. Any first-year psychology student would label this escapist behaviour, and some might add that living terrifying experiences vicariously is one way of exorcising fear. It is also a very powerful way of proving to audiences that the here and now is perfectly idyllic compared with the wild and terrible things lurking out there. Virtually everyone sitting in the audience is better off than the victims on the screen. Together we shiver on cue at the simulated horror, comforted by the thought that it isn't really happening. For Americans, and for those of us living safely within their orbit, no invasion of killer sharks or body-snatchers is likely to get us. And, God forbid, should the unthinkable actually occur, those ingenious, courageous police, fire fighters and scientists can surely be relied upon to defend us.

In other words, despite the fascination with make-believe futures and pasts, the real preoccupation is irrevocably in the present. The past is only a prelude to the present and was never very perfect anyway, and the future is fraught with seen and unseen dangers; so what we have right now may be the best we can ever hope for. Beside future plague, famine, nuclear war or the return of the ice age, the present is paradise. Rather than learning from the past or preparing for the future, we are encouraged to lie back and be entertained by them.

It is our view, however, that the past is something we are all responsible for; and the future is there for us to invent. If human society is neither the offspring of history nor a machine run by progress, but the creation of people out of a galaxy of possibilities, then the importance of the social imagination is self-evident; it is the guide for change and evolution. As Castoriadis phrases it in a 1979 article in *Sociologie et sociétés*, societies, like people, are mortal; some die young, some live long past their time.

> Death [of a society] is not necessarily or usually instantaneous; and its relationship to the new life, for which it may be a precondition, is each time a new enigma. The "decline of the West" is an old theme and, in a profound way, false. For the slogan masks the possibilities of a new world that the decomposition of the West may set free, and it ignores the potential of this world by covering over a political affair with a botanical metaphor . . . . We are not interested in establishing whether this flower will wither, whether it is withering or has already withered. We want to understand what is dying in this socio-historical world, how it is dying and possibly why. And we want also to discover, if possible, what is in the process of being born. (our translation)

Well, certainly we can be fairly sure that the great revolution prophesied by nineteenth-century critics of capitalism like Marx, which has not happened so far, probably will not happen. And where revolution has triumphed, there is no guarantee that humane and enlightened civilization follows. Consequently, both Eastern and Western versions of the good society are steadily losing credibility, even among the formerly faithful. People everywhere are growing sceptical and more boldly insistent that they must think and speak for themselves. There are strong currents in the political upheavals of our day that do indeed say that a transformation is underway.

Chapter 4

Reinventing the Future

Our excursion into the territory of culture and modern-day empire has thus far led us to one great realization: industrially advanced societies are beset with tremendous inner conflicts that actually overshadow the economic upheavals we are now experiencing. The malaise goes far too deep to be passed off simply as a reaction against bad times. It was, after all, in the Sixties — the decade when capitalism was at the peak of its performance — that so many liberation movements were launched and citizen-action politics was introduced. People discovered that affluence was no sure cure for discrimination and disadvantage. Even the self-satisfied middle classes found that two cars and a mortgage-free bungalow couldn't keep the kids from dropping out and turning on. They, too, began to worry about the quality of life.

In 1964 UNESCO took up the cause of cultural rights, returning to a clause in the 1948 Universal Declaration of Human Rights and attempting to put flesh on the idea through a series of international studies and conferences on cultural policy. (Article 27 of that document reads, in part: "Everyone has the right to freely participate in the cultural life of the community, to enjoy the arts and to share in scientific advancement and its benefits; everyone has the right to the protection of the moral and material interests resulting from any scientific, literary or artistic production of which he is the author.") However, the cause of cultural rights was bound to have a very different significance for countries of the Third World than for Western nations.

During the Fifties and Sixties, the emerging countries, many of them ex-colonies of ex-empires, had begun to make their collective presence felt in world politics. Declining to throw their lot in with either the East or the West, a number of them began meeting as a group of non-aligned states in the early Seventies. Their debut as a power bloc was heralded by the call for a new international economic order (NIEO) – in reality the demand for a radical rearrangement of economic and industrial power. In 1974, the United Nations adopted a resolution and an action plan for the establishment of the NIEO, opening what the West has somewhat euphemistically dubbed the North–South dialogue. Such a vote would have been unthinkable twenty years ago; but in 1974 it reflected the shift of UNESCO from a passive, pro-West agency to an activist, pro-development and Third World–oriented organization. It also reflects the reality that there are more poor countries suffering the injustices of domination than there are rich ones enjoying the fruits of dominating. Needless to say, Western countries were shocked by the turn of events. The United States actually withheld its UNESCO dues for a couple of years in protest. But the die was cast.

As the information age dawned, developing countries began to recognize that economic disparity is intimately related to inequalities in the handling and distribution of information and knowledge. The demand for a new economic order was quickly followed by a parallel demand for a new world information order. Analyses subsequently conducted by UNESCO of the flow of communications world-wide (focusing particularly on television programming and news services) revealed a staggering lopsidedness. The majority of countries, it found, are consumers, not producers, of information and are therefore not in a position to contribute to any real two-way exchange. Most of them act as the mute receivers of other peoples' messages, even where those messages concern their own country and society. Given the bias of the countries that own and control most of the world's communications systems, news about developing nations and their social problems are, to put it delicately, infrequent. UNESCO figured that eighty per cent of the world's news emanates from the major news agencies (Reuters, AP, UPI and the others) but that only twenty per cent of the coverage deals with the Third World, where fully three-quarters of all humanity lives. Moreover,the same handful of industrially advanced nations that write most of the messages also design and manufacture the equipment used in telecommunications and thus dominate the international commerce in both hardware and software. The only way most nations can even contemplate joining the information age and finding a way to get a word in edgeways, as it were, is to import the technology along with the programs—American colour TV along with *Dallas*. Understandably, many people in developing nations feel this situation only serves to reinforce old colonial attitudes and dependencies and, in the long run, impede social and cultural development.

During the last decade, UNESCO became the chief forum for the debate over the new world information order. What began as an innocuous discussion about the means by which nation-states could make their artistic and intellectual heritage available to their citizens suddenly turned into a highly charged political skirmish that took Western members of the UN by surprise. In 1976, when it looked like the Nineteenth General Assembly of UNESCO was heading for a sudden-death confrontation between the East and the West, a commission was set up under Sean MacBride (the founder of Amnesty International) to study international communications problems.

Four years later, at the Twenty-first Assembly, the MacBride report was accepted amid stormy debate, and an International Programme for the Development of Communications was put into place. By hard negotiation, Western delegations were able to contain the issue, but not to soften the determination of the Third World to gain greater control over their economic and cultural affairs. There can be no illusions about what this involves: a departure forever from the ideology, enshrined in UNESCO since the Forties, that champions the "free flow of information." Today most of the world worries not about free flow, but about *balanced* flow.

Meanwhile, in Canada, the idea of cultural policy caught hold of the bureaucratic imagination. With a well-established tradition of public subsidy for cultural activity through a number of semi-autonomous agencies (the CBC, the NFB and so on), it was an easy step for government to convince itself to assume a larger role fashioning and co-ordinating policy. For along with cultural policy came the notion of cultural development, and further, the possibility of governments having responsibility for its care and keeping. The old custom of passive patronage gave way to federally initiated programs and projects, and deep within the department of the secretary of state, small empires began a-building.

However, the discovery of cultural policy by the Trudeau government in its first flush of power was solely on the level of domestic social policy, related primarily to the arts though extended, bit by bit, to include the cultural industries. Despite the explosion of telecommunications world-wide and the linking of culture to issues of human rights and national sovereignty, issues that burst onto the international stage with unexpected force in the mid-Seventies, cultural policy here was never related to external affairs. It continues to be treated as a domestic concern, whose only foreign implication has to do with transborder trade relations with the United States.

So there culture sits: at the bottom of every politician's agenda, poorly thought of and poorly thought through as a public issue. The result is a history of public involvement in cultural affairs with a pitifully inadequate rationale for that involvement. We have wads of worthy rhetoric in the Broadcasting Act and in the statutes establishing the Canada Council, the National Arts Centre and so forth, but few down-to-earth definitions of their purpose. Consequently, the recurring bouts of culture-bashing—from parliamentary back-benchers critical of grants going to poets who use scatological language, from members of the public offended by modern sculpture outside federal buildings and from Cabinet itself, habitually furious with the CBC—go on virtually unchallenged.

Under fire, cultural agencies seem weak, given to ineffectual, defensive behaviour that seems moth-like in its flirtation with oblivion. For within the bureaucracy it is apparently sufficient to invoke excellence, public edification, national unity or some such undisputed and ill-defined good; cultural policy, like art itself, is assumed to be its own defence. So the intelligent and the intelligible arguments have not been forthcoming when justifications have been demanded. Far from clarifying anything, the report of the Applebaum-Hébert Committee, with its grab-bag approach to intellectual discussion, only added to the confusion.

Ordinary folks and the uninitiated are still waiting for someone to explain why the Canada Council should matter to them. The answers they are given have the consistency of marshmallow and are bland enough to suit any philosophy. This may help slip a project through the machinery of government decision-making, but it is worse than useless when someone on the outside wants a serious accounting. How do you measure excellence? How can you tell a good cultural policy from a failed one? As it is not axiomatic that all cultural policies are unmitigated successes, and as it is possible to imagine programs that are counter-productive or even harmful to the cultural ecology, we obviously need to devise better definitions of what we mean and what we want by way of cultural development.

In a remarkable essay in *Sociologie et sociétés* on "the idea of cultural development," Fernand Dumont (who was closely involved in the preparation of Quebec's 1978 White Paper on cultural policy) reaches beneath the fashionable surface of the term to ask, pointedly, whose culture is being referred to and why a need to develop it is felt. In the first place, he states, most cultural policies have sought to do the same thing: encourage the *production* of culture and its *consumption* by the population. Whether in the arts, education or broadcasting, the model used is industrial and presupposes a culture consisting of organizations employing workers who produce commodities for sale. These structures, then, are what require development.

But development itself is a loaded word, owing much to ideologies of progress and the imperative of change. Whatever the object of its attentions, development contrives some sort of progression; from one state to another (presumably better) one, though planners rarely stop to wonder whether the institutions built into the first state are in themselves adequate or appropriate.

For instance, cultural development as it is usually envisaged does not relate the production of cultural goods to the culture as it is lived and experienced by people. As Dumont would phrase it, this kind of cultural development dealt only with "prescribed" culture (what industry brings to market) and turns a blind eye to the general condition of the environment. He maintains that "lived" culture (or popular culture, as we have called it) has been bled dry by commercial culture. Common knowledge has lost out to expertise, and cultural activity that isn't planned or produced by professionals is scarcely recognized as such. Usually it is discounted as recreation or social therapy.

Meanwhile, mass culture and élite culture, passing for the sum total of what is meant by culture, have evolved highly sophisticated forms that have lost touch with popular culture and no longer depend on the active participation of an audience, or even its live presence. "From now on," Dumont concludes, "a radical reversal of the perspective lying at the heart of all conceptions and policies to do with cultural development is essential [our translation]."

In his essay Dumont alludes to the fact that our society is busily churning out all manner of symbolic goods as well as material goods. Whether this production is controlled by private corporations or state institutions matters little when it comes to the reality that most of our population consumes symbolic goods made elsewhere. And herein is the ambiguity still plaguing our critique.

Living as we do on the edge of the metropolitan United States of America, there can be no doubt that the state has to intercede — but how? Are there not dangers that such measures, however necessary for the public well-being, will simply reinforce the power of the state and encourage technocrats to barge into one of the most delicate areas of human life? Certainly it is worrisome to anyone who feels that domination and dependence demand concerted action. It is equally problematic for those who want to see the creation of a more democratic society in which powers appropriated by the state would be redistributed back to the communities of citizens whence they originally came. Though we are anxious to see a national government strong enough to confront the US, this strength must not be used to sanction excessive centralization at the hands of federal or provincial mandarins.

In the case of culture, we particularly have to fear state intervention that interprets cultural development as a projection of economic development. The reason is elucidated by Northrop Frye in *Divisions on a Ground*, his 1982 collection of essays on Canadian culture:

> Culture movements are different in direction and rhythm from political and economic ones. Politically and economically the current of history is towards greater unity, and unity in this context includes uniformity. Technology is the most dramatic aspect of this development: one cannot take off in a jet plane and expect a radically different way of life in the place where the plane lands. But culture has something vegetable about it, something that increasingly needs to grow from roots, something that demands a small region and a restricted locale.

The pressure of economic and political development thus moves toward centralization and hierarchical structure, toward uniformity and against the diversity that is the life-blood of culture.

At issue here is whether the model of the consumer society that prevails in the sphere of material goods — a few producing for mass consumption — can be applied to symbolic goods as well; whether the rank-and-file members of the mass (all of us, actually) are to go on functioning as "targets" for a marketing strategy, there to take what some industry has placed on the supermarket shelf.

If culture is what gives *sense* to life, to human society and nature, why then should this sense be produced only by specialized agencies — schools, industry and the mass media? The answer, of course, is that it shouldn't be. More to the point, it cannot be. Mass culture cannot substitute for popular culture, at least not without entirely transforming it. The division of life and culture — an extension of the division of labour invented by the industrial revolution — may have opened the way for improvements in social justice, but the price has been dear. By British historian Francis Hearn's calculation, the price has been the loss by the working class of its own secular culture, this being the trade-off for integration into the bourgeois mainstream. On a day-to-day level, the alienation experienced by industrial workers has more to do with their cultural impoverishment, Hearn maintains, than with theories about ownership of production, however illuminating.

But whether we want to talk about the ownership of production, for the sake of Canadians or the workers (or both), there is no disputing their cultural rights — in this case the freedom to formulate an interpretation of reality and the world and to construct a set of values that will lend sense to their lives. This means putting an end to what Dumont calls the censorship of popular culture, a censorship that comes about through the combined force of the experts, supported by bourgeois ideology.

Eradication of this censorship has nothing to do with nostalgia for Grandpa's rocking chair. Nor should it be confused with a simplistic notion of "the people," some abstract proletariat, expected to fulfil a destiny as the cat's-paw of ambitious humbugs and dictators.

But what if cultural development were to concern itself with popular culture and its rehabilitation, drawing on its positive attributes and remaining strengths? This is Dumont's point. "What popular cultures retain is their own unique way of life, their sense of shared responsibilities with neighbours and family, and the ties they have between daily life and culture. Herein lies the promise. Not in resurrections of the past, or folkloric theatre, but in social changes whereby culture would assume weight and importance."

This sort of cultural development steers a course very far removed from those puerile "culturisms" governments are fond of promoting. Take, for example, the scheme hatched by Gérard Pelletier when he was secretary of state between 1968 and 1972 to democratize and decentralize the arts, so people across the country would have access to the treasures of Canadian culture. Cultural democracy in this instance, however, would only grant citizens a share in the cultural inheritance of the nation and a right to benefit from activities that until recently had been reserved for the upper classes, but that are now supported by the public purse. Pelletier's democratization didn't mention popular culture, much less anything about the accountability of existing cultural institutions to the public. It was only concerned with distributing an already determined set of cultural artifacts — production and consumption again. It was a policy of disseminating a few more material comforts and symbolic goods, while existing political and economic systems carry on unscathed. In this vision of things, cultural development follows meekly in the path of economic development.

Obviously, this is not the kind of solution that interests us. Citizens and communities will not be able to take back responsibility for their lives if they stop here. Political theories that only consider economics and ignore culture, as we have said, won't solve the crisis either. Unfortunately, when we look to the traditional Left for enlightenment on the subject, we are bound for disappointment yet again; for there, too, we encounter little interest and not much sympathy. It is curious, but often those who align themselves with "the people" and express solicitude for their cause turn out themselves to be élitist when it comes to culture. Even Bertolt Brecht could state, in his writings on theatre:

> The history of falsehoods hidden in the term "popular" is a long and complex one, scarred by social struggle. Remembering these conflicts, we can say that we need a popular art, meaning an art

destined for the people ... for the "people themselves" who *produce*, and who have, for so long,
been the object of politics and who now must
become the subject. (our translation)

In other words, according to Brecht, the people who are
about to become the subject of politics will dutifully become
the subject matter of culture, too—always the spectators,
never the creators. Those who produce the economic wealth
will finally get to share in it, but they will only be allowed
to share precariously in the expression of culture.

Closer to home, the New Democratic Party offers us a
latter-day example of the same attitude. Following Prime
Minister Trudeau's spectacular $2-billion budget cut in 1978,
when it became apparent that the largest slice would be hacked
out of cultural budgets, an *ad hoc* committee known as the
1812 Committee immediately sprang into being to protest the
Draconian treatment of the arts. While rallies and public
meetings were taking place in cities across the country, a
delegation of well-known artists showed up in Ottawa to
confront the politicians. Hastily the House of Commons
declared it National Arts Day, and all three party leaders
agreed to meet the group. That day Ed Broadbent dismissed
the 1812 Committee as a pack of opportunists who had shown
little concern for the economic hardships of other working
Canadians, and who were only bothering to complain because
their own livelihoods were in jeopardy. Broadbent was
subsequently taken to task in *This Magazine* by playwright
Rick Salutin for his insinuation that:

the problems of Canadian culture and its makers
hold no special interest from the point of view of
Canadian workers .... As if that entire area of
human experience can be left in the exclusive and
tender care of the Canadian bourgeoisie who
presumably *are* interested in it. As if the working
class might care only—or overwhelmingly—about
jobs, and bread and butter and not about the
intellectual and imaginative content of their lives
and that of the country.

Indeed, Broadbent's remarks not only displayed a terrible
misunderstanding of human society; they revealed a contempt
for the working class, which, as Salutin said, "is a human

reality, not an economic category, and its members have cultural needs, not just economic ones."

Since then the NDP has made several attempts to develop a cultural policy, though it still lags far behind the Conservatives in terms of the care and attention given the task. The party brass have, at least, tried to tidy up its public image. References to disappearing Canadian talent and endangered cultural resources crept into speeches during the federal election campaigns of 1979 and 1980, often in the same breath as comments about the need to repatriate the economy. Nevertheless the story reveals a nasty quirk of the Canadian Left, which typically suffers artists about as gladly as company spies.

Philip Resnick, for example, in his otherwise balanced account of class and nationalism in English Canada, backs off at the sight of an artist, leaving a strong whiff of class suspicion wafting through his book *Land of Cain*. He slots artists and creators, as self-employed professionals, in with the petty bourgeoisie and states that their opinions on nationalism (which apparently don't count for much anyway) range "from those who saw both nationalism and the state as a fillip to their own ambitions (e.g. writers and artists) to those professionals allied with large multinational corporations."

In other words, artists are either egomaniacs or sell-outs. The nationalist writer or film-maker is someone who acts out of pure self-interest, and what gives the lie to any professed political commitment is the fact that creators could gain financially were Canadian books or films to get proper distribution in Canada and find a popular audience. This rule, however, does not apply to nationalist farmers or fishermen, who for all their difficulties usually make a far better living than writers and film-makers. Curiously, Resnick asks "to what extent English Canadian intellectuals, including academics, [have] created the new nationalism as their confreres did in Quebec in the early 1960s .... or to what extent were they themselves merely responding to a political force let loose by the waning influence of the United States;" but he does not hang around for an answer. He also mentions, but does not examine, the evolution of cultural nationalism and its politicizing role within the cultural community.

Because Marxists have by and large accepted the élite definition of culture uncritically and identified it with the exclusive pursuits of the bourgeoisie, they have tended to see artists as opportunists, not workers, making a living by flattering capitalists and selling them useless luxuries. This is the same myopia that led Russia's Bolsheviks to become the new czars, promoting and enshrining an art and culture every bit as backward as that which flattered and glorified the Romanoffs. But there is an anomaly here, for while overlooking culture as a basis for political action, the Left does acknowledge the enormous political importance of the mass media, the modern "opiate of the masses."

The shaky understanding of culture has furthermore led some Leftists to attack the nationalist position. Debi Wells and Steve Moore, for example—in a collection of essays called *Imperialism, Nationalism and Canada*, published by the Marxist Institute of Canada—try to take out the kingpin in economic nationalist theory by marshalling facts and figures to prove that if Canada is deindustrializing, so is the United States. The decline of manufacturing, they argue, is an international trend in the imperialist world; capitalism is the main problem. Their approach leads them on the absurd mission of proving that US domination doesn't exist (or doesn't matter?) because the Americans' own economic performance is slipping. In effect, they send in narrow-minded socialism to do battle with narrow nationalism. In the hair-splitting that ensues, it never seems to occur to Wells and Moore that deindustrialization is not the only way of measuring the effect of imperialism, here or anywhere else. They simply use capitalism's own arguments to paint themselves into a corner.

This sort of piecemeal approach clearly has failed us. The times and the interconnectedness of the crisis we face as a civilization demand a global perspective. Because Canadian nationalists have concentrated on economic analysis in its conventional form (that is, without taking account of the cultural dimension), the relevance of Americanization to other social ills has been left unexplored. The national unity debate has dwelt almost exclusively these past twenty years on the Canada–Quebec dichotomy (although the focus is now shifting to the West–East split), and the question of US involvement in Canadian life is meanwhile scarcely mentioned.

In his book *Dominance and Dependency*, John Hutcheson identifies three main sources of tension in Canadian society: the binational and bilingual nature of the country, the relations of the regions and their provincial governments with the central government, and the relations between Canada and the United States. Hutcheson examines only the latter, although not because he believes the other two less important. Still, just lining up these three contradictions invites comparisons. They can, for instance, be viewed as three different but complementary issues. The Quebec–Canada, two nations–two languages tension represents a cultural contradiction; the regions versus Ottawa a political one; and Canada–US relations primarily an economic one. If our ambition is not just to describe such contradictions but to overcome them, we should perhaps first recognize that they impinge on each other and, in the long run, cannot be taken separately. For as long as we try to treat them as local injuries, unrelated to any endemic disease, we aren't likely to find satisfactory solutions. We may fail to take notice of the flaws imprinted in the fabric of society itself.

Examining the nationalist analyses of Canada's and Quebec's economies, we often find the criticism of American domination boils down to resentment for the way it forestalls autonomous industrial development here. Apparently accepting the metropolitan mode, critics simply stake out the right to "do it ourselves" without changing any of the essentials. Documents such as the reports of the Applebaum-Hébert committee and of the Pepin-Robarts task force, which gloss over the entire matter of economic and cultural domination by the United States, are usually forced to extremes. Applebert counselled severe restrictions on government involvement in culture (particularly in areas where profits are to be made), even though public support has always been the mainstay of Canadian culture; Pepin-Robarts recommended the virtual balkanization of Canada. Notwithstanding the extraordinary experience of travelling about the country, listening to Canadians and Quebeckers expressing their hopes and fears for their nations *A Future Together* reported only that it was an "incredible journey in quest of a country" and never tells us what the quest turned up. Likewise, Applebert bypassed the heart and soul of the cultural issue, and as a result, its report is equally statist and abstract, written in undigestible bureaucratese.

We know, however, that our society has inherited massive problems that present us with a horrifying inventory of symptoms—the energy crisis, the food crisis, the economic crisis, the toxic waste crisis, the nuclear arms crisis—that add up to big trouble for Western civilization. Our conclusion, as we have said, is to insist on viewing society as one entity made up of interconnecting parts, where culture, politics and economics are subplots in a larger story; this means we should be looking for a social theory, a social strategy that embraces them all.

Of course, this is not a particularly startling or even new suggestion. Academics, politicians and experts may have one-track minds, but the rebels in our midst have certainly understood that fundamental social change doesn't happen by joining a political party or writing reports for government committees.

But the revolution the Sixties spoke of was less about theory than about how to live, how to organize and how to act politically. The new society was to begin with ourselves and the revolution was to be more than just talk. Telling the story of that generation in *Long Way From Home*, Myrna Kostash writes:

> The human being is not just an economic and political construct; the human being is also a psychic and cultural event, and the revolution that will liberate us is the one that will expel the oppression not only from the workplace but from the personality as well. The fact is that we are mutilated people condemned to the intellectual, emotional and spiritual life of the marketplace, and only the revolution can heal us, the revolution that implicates all our comings and goings, all our busy little doings, all the private fastnesses in which we cower and make believe we are happy . . . . The cultural life of the revolution, then, is the imagining, in embryo, of the personality and the lifestyle of the liberated future.

The legacy of the Sixties isn't only a style of politics that has come down to us in the Eighties as single-issue activism. Its most valuable achievement was the release of the social imagination, the emancipation of people's expectations—not for higher wages, as Pierre Trudeau would have us believe, but for a better way of living. It made people realize they could invent their own future. And now, whatever the particular issue or demand, the voices from the cheap seats are ever-present and getting louder. The tactics may vary in detail from one issue to the next, but taking all in all, there is one common denominator: people are not content to go on delegating the decision-making to others, be it a government, a dictator or a husband.

Their call is for justice and *autonomy*, the return of power — as the slogan goes — to the people.

We could say that our collective goals are now largely determined by the cumulative processes of society: economic growth and technological development. Given that the ideology and goals of advanced capitalism are firmly imbedded in its mode of production, we can expect the first requirement of socialization to be to develop the *normal* person, which is to say the "well-adjusted" individual who can produce and consume as society prescribes. Balance is a key concept, for high-tech society favours adaptation and the statistically average, basing its understanding of the social sciences on the idea that individuals ought to adjust to society at all costs in order to preserve the *status quo*. According to the German biologist Kurt Goldstein, an adapted existence can still be a sick one — for example, the domesticated animal that manages somehow to make do in a restricted environment but would not survive if released back into the "natural" environment. The healthy individual, he says, "is not normal but *normative*, and is capable of creating and assuming his or her own norms. Thus the externally directed individual prized by industrial societies has to be replaced by the autonomous individuals who will be able to base their identity and behaviour on values they define and assume themselves [our translation]."

We are not promoting here a new-and-improved brand of moral rearmament in the belief that all we need do is reform individuals one by one in order to transform society. On the contrary, we recognize that institutions as well as individuals require alteration and that whatever social organization we devise will inevitably correspond to a particular social character. In other words, the two — character and *modus operandi* — are enmeshed in each other. Again, to be precise about the terms we are using, the autonomous society — as distinct from the heteronomous society, which receives its laws and orders from another — is self-directed, able to make decisions and carry them out without deferring to external influence. The accepted and most common use of the word conveys the idea of non-dependence and self-determination. Taken to an unhealthy extreme, however, autonomy can turn into autonomization (not to be confused with automation), signifying a radical isolation whereby individuals are separated and estranged from others around them in a way that only hermits or vegetables could find comfortable. Autonomization is a form of alienation, the great theme of Marxist literature that has traditionally focused on the disjunction between the co-operative social effort of production and private ownership of industry—a disjunction that, in the colonies, translates into the conflict between the native population and a foreign ruling class that owns the means of production.

The failure of both capitalism and socialism as practicable and just schemes for social organization (as well as the odd congruence between the two systems as they have evolved) invites the brave and determined to go back to revising basic assumptions. This critical position, which sees similarities in the oppressive bureaucracy created by state capitalism in the East and private enterprise capitalism in the West, has already opened new paths for evaluating both ideologies. In Europe one prolific line of inquiry grew out of the Left's disenchantment with socialism "as it really exists" (to use the East German philosopher Rudolf Bahro's phrase) and catalogues its shortcomings in an effort to establish where it went wrong.

In his 1979 book *L'Alternative*, Bahro rejects the official doctrine of socialist countries by reinstating human conscience, subjectivity and culture as motive forces of history, phenomena that have for so long been discounted as mere shadows of more important realities, with no real life or influence of their own. By taking this stand, Bahro follows in the footsteps of Herbert Marcuse, who began to define himself as a cultural Marxist after writing *Soviet Marxism* in 1948, when he broke away from the purely economic interpretation of history. Reviewing *L'Alternative* in *Les temps modernes* just before he died, Marcuse wrote:

> The inertia and weakness of the masses, their dependence, expressed in capitalist countries as the dichotomy between people and the dominating class, and in socialist countries as the dichotomy between people and the bureaucracy, leads to the autonomization of the power elite. [Bahro] is persuaded that this will be thwarted only when a different sort of organization is introduced. (our translation)

The form of organization alluded to is *autogestion*, a term fairly widely used in Europe that refers to a method of collective organization based on principles of local control and co-operative endeavour.

Originally *autogestion* was understood in socialist circles and more particularly in working-class politics to mean, quite literally, self-management: factories would, in time, be directed and managed by the worker-employees themselves, by the producers of wealth rather than the accumulators of wealth. In France and several other European countries, the idea resulted in experimentation with industrial democracy, from worker-controlled plants to employee representation on the board of directors.

But as an idea or principle of self-development, *autogestion* obviously had applications to other situations besides the workplace, and eventually the idea was expanded to embrace a general theory of social life and organization. Worker management is, after all, the outcome of a rearrangement of power and the mechanisms of decision-making in a plant. In fact, of course, the self-managed enterprise is not new, though it has experienced something of a come-back recently (in the form of co-ops, communes, storefront social services and so forth) as a part of the Sixties experiment. But one can identify principles that are essentially *autogestionnaire* in the organizational (non-hierarchic, democratic) tactics being consciously applied by many contemporary community groups.

According to Bahro and others, *autogestion* still had to be rescued from the economic sphere because, as an idea, it is community-oriented and takes the whole range of social activity and everyday life in its purview. Moreover, the old supposition of Marxists that there is an automatic harmony between theory and practice, between logic and history, is now discredited. We have learned, finally, that each individual and each group is a subject of history and not just a member of the proletariat. Subjectivity and conscience can therefore be resurrected and injected back into the debate.

In capitalist countries, the other cliché, that the good life is a pot of gold lying at the end of raw economic development and unlimited technological progress, is losing ground just as fast. While in Poland, farmers demand the right to have their own union, in Canada, women are prepared to set up illegal clinics to provide safe abortions to which they are legally entitled but that the medical profession won't provide. People are reaching out to take back responsibility for themselves and their lives instead of delegating it to experts, civil servants or party headquarters.

But this phenomenon raises a very perplexing point. Why is it that large collectivities of people have historically been willing to renounce their autonomy in favour of a small group, who have then taken over the running of things? How do we account for this abdication of power, be it voluntary or exacted by force?

In Marcuse's intellectual tradition, known as the Frankfort School, emancipation is the central idea; its meaning is derived from the legal definition (a child's release from the tutelage of parents) denoting the acquisition of autonomy. So autonomy or independence is not absolute; it is comparative and assumes significance in relation to others.

But still, how are we to explain the fact that throughout history, people have been constrained to accept conditions of dependence, often despite the grave disadvantages? Bahro and Marcuse speak of compensation. A person forgoes emancipation in exchange for the security that the ruling class, the company, the empire or the block bully can provide. The feudal warlord defends the serf against other feudal warlords; the bourgeoisie develops the forces of production so that everyone can benefit; the empire maintains order — civilization — against the barbarian hordes beyond its boundaries. For women, it was the lace ghetto in exchange for male protection and economic security. And ironically, we are given the same pitch for accepting US domination: it's the price we must pay for a comfortable standard of living and military protection against the Communist threat.

Rulers and ruling classes everywhere can, of course, be trusted to exploit and manipulate the situation abroad for political gain at home. Foreign policy is always an extension of domestic politics, and presumably, for countries lower down in the pecking order, the trade-off for subservience to the farmyard heavies is protection from the villainies of outside superpowers and aggressors.

In the United States, Cold War fear-mongering came back into style with Ronald Reagan, who loves to tell Americans stories of how the Russians are lying and cheating their way toward the Persian Gulf and into Central America. In Russia, it's the fear of American encirclement that is served up to chill the population. From either perspective, the "other side" is painted in hostile, menacing and duplicitous tones. Of course, this affords a wonderful opportunity for leaders of both mega-nations to reinstate virginity and to justify all sorts of gulags in the name of national security. Even an apprehended external threat can be the occasion for beefing up the power of the central authority; this only increases the odds that young men will be sent abroad once again to sacrifice their lives in places like Afghanistan and the Middle East. It is also a good excuse for taming the rebels at home, purging the "enemies lurking within." For Jews in the Soviet Union and blacks in the United States, the message is the same: there will be few deals in justice this year; dissidents and national minorities beware.

Despite everything, we have seen a rise in recent years in the number of non-aligned countries refusing to swear fealty to either superpower because they find the cost exorbitant. Others are only waiting for a propitious moment to resign from the empire. And inside the empires, too, people are demanding an end to the dependence on big government, big business and big unions, and they are resisting the erosion of their freedom in all spheres. The parallels are not coincidental. We believe that internal and external domination are a pair following the same logic; a logic founded on the domination of nature. As nature is exploited and its laws decoded (supposedly for the benefit of "all mankind"), a system of production is set up that eventually leads to the gross manipulation of people as well as the environment. Eventually, everything under capitalism becomes a commodity. This is why Lenin called imperialism the ultimate form of capitalism, seeing it as the logical outcome of domination and dependence stretched *ad absurdum*. Hence it will be necessary to confront the values and behaviour of imperialism, which is to say the assumptions and principles lying at the heart of societies who practise it.

For us this suggests, first of all, cultural reform. The cycle of human and natural destruction will not be broken merely by rejecting the empire to carry on doing business and conducting our affairs the same way. As Bahro states, "The elimination of this state of subordination is the only way to cope with the proliferation of material goods . . . . [A] cultural revolution is necessary if we are to break out of the all-embracing economic dynamic and bring mankind back into balance with nature [our translation]." Bahro's point is that the only way out of the morass is for us to deal with our addiction to economic growth and its endless stream of gadgetry and bogus necessity.

Not surprisingly, authorities of the German Democratic Republic took Bahro's ideas extremely seriously; as the cover notes on the French translation of his book tell it, Bahro was arrested in 1977 after giving an interview to West German television on the eve of the publication of his work there, and subsequently condemned in a secret trial to prison, where he languished for four years. Those who might want to interpret

Bahro's thesis as a desire to put advanced capitalism in the place of socialism should take heed, for, as Marcuse perceived so well, Bahro denounces both regimes. Were that not so, he could have defected and chosen exile in the West over incarceration.

Returning to the idea of *autogestion* and non-subordination, we must underline another important break in traditional attitudes toward nature. As more and more of us are coming to understand, it really isn't safe to fool with Mother Nature or to treat her as something to be tamed or used up. We are beginning to see the wisdom of our native forbears, who knew they had to respect and live in harmony with nature or risk destruction; being a part of nature, they saw it is not possible for man to despoil nature without despoiling humankind. Historians have pointed out that whenever human society has taken a sharp turn in a new direction, it has typically been accompanied by an altered concept of nature—and the usual end-of-the-world predictions. This leads us to suppose that we may be now experiencing the dawn of a cultural mutation presaged by an altered awareness of nature.

The environmentalist movement points us in the direction of self-determination and *autogestion* in that it puts great value on the individual and collective responsibility for conservation. This most certainly goes against the cultural ethos of modern industry. To say this is also to realize that these new beliefs and practices are bound to conflict with the dominant institutions, the conformist mentality and the huge vested interests of those sitting atop the vertical mosaic. Nevertheless, if it is true that the cultural revolution has already begun, it means, as Antonio Gramsci said, that the representation of reality and the values that bind the elements of society into a whole have already begun to crack and flake off.

For those of us who do not want to accommodate the *status quo* and who have lost confidence in the experts (indeed, in all of the panaceas offered so far), it may just be that we can make do without a glamorous utopia. We might begin by taking back our autonomy and exercising it in all aspects of life. This means refuting the idea of progress, which Western society has dined out on for centuries. People must take responsibility for their own nature as human beings before appropriating nature; this must be the central consideration on which all else hinges. It also means that politics must subsume economics and lead us to distinguish between three aspects of human society— civil society, political society and the state. (Political society in this context is the political culture practised by citizens outside of government and party politics.)

It may well be that liberal and socialist societies of the late twentieth century have already arrived at the limits of their possibility. Besides, if we agree with the French political scientist Pierre Rosanvallon that Marx is the true heir of Adam Smith, we will not be surprised that Bahro's critique of socialism parallels Marcuse's of advanced capitalism. Rosanvallon expounds his thesis in *Le Capitalisme utopique*, concluding, as the title suggests, that Marxism is but a utopian form of capitalism and as such is based on the same set of flawed assumptions about human society. To arrive at his provocative association of Smith and Marx, Rosanvallon first establishes that Smith was more than the eighteenth-century prophet of the bourgeoisie and modern capitalism; he was the author of an economic theory that, in fact, differs substantially from that which came to be the ideology of capitalism.

For in Smith, it is not the economy that defines and propels society, but society that determines the economy. The market is described as a mechanism of social organization rather than as an economic regulator, which is how Smith has commonly been misread. Rosanvallon offers this insight: "Liberalism as an ideology of the market implicates itself in the battle for the de-territorialization of the economy and the construction of a fluid, homogeneous space structured only by the geography of price [our translation]." Liberalism, in other words, thinks of economics as an abstract, detached from nations and the temporal concerns of real communities. Money, as the saying goes, knows no nationality. Economics has its own internal logic, which governments and mere mortals dare not tamper with. Of course, the transnational corporation is the agent *par excellence* for deterritorializing not just the economy but culture and politics as well.

Perhaps two hundred years after Jeremy Bentham predicted "the test of the wealth of nations will be to produce an international 'culture' which transcends all political divisions ... [where] the market becomes the new common patria of all humanity," it is coming to pass.

According to Rosanvallon, Marx confuses the practice of nineteenth-century capitalism with liberal ideology, thereby allying himself closely with Smith's fundamental belief. For both Smith and Marx have in the back of their minds an idea of a pre-existing and self-sufficient civil society that delegates its autonomy to the state. In its ideal form, this society becomes "transparent" in the sense that it becomes so simple that there is no practical need for politics. With liberalism, the market (Smith's famous "unseen hand") is society's guiding principle; government is reduced to a minimum and society goes on automatic pilot, leaving everything to the immutable laws of business and the marketplace. In Marx's utopia, by comparison, all political institutions become useless because scarcity vanishes and abundance makes it possible for each to receive according to his or her needs. In order to reach this Shangri-La, it is still necessary for capitalism to evolve first, to accomplish its historical mission of leading the world to abundance. Marx predicts that once communism is achieved, however, the state and the law will fade away.

In both utopias, we can see, the vaunted transparent society comes about through the disappearance of politics. Only, contrary to predictions, the state hasn't dwindled or withered; rather it has abrogated more and more power unto itself, swallowing up political life. Politics have become the creation and the creature of government and the party. Citizens who take it into their heads to act outside the carefully delineated arena are bound to be damned and labelled dissidents or extraparliamentary agitators. Thus, says Rosanvallon:

> To be emancipated from utopian liberalism is to think of the political aspect of society in its role as a companion to both civil society and the state; it is to autonomize and particularize the political field, not to dissolve it; because democracy can only develop where there is unshakeable recognition that social division and conflicts are unavoidable; it is to understand that democracy is a battle never done, that it never overcomes all its difficulties and achieves all its goals, that it is not a transitory reality. It is, in a word, to return to politics.

For Rosanvallon, reinstating politics means defrocking liberalism and rooting out its influences wherever they hide.

> It is not enough to denounce the malfunctioning of the market economy, proceeding with a "scientific" analysis that nevertheless assumes the logic of capitalism. Liberalism is not reduceable to a simple economic doctrine of *laissez-faire*. At a much more profound level it represents both the political and the social sides of society, and paradoxically it is

recognizable in social theories usually taken to be antagonistic. It is, in effect, the common root from which most of the modern representations of society have sprung, which is why, in my eyes, Marx is the heir of Adam Smith.

It seems to us that any new approach has to pay attention to civil and political society as well as to the state. For one thing, the most pressing item on the agenda for Canada and Quebec is being ignored. In recent years, the Quebec question has forced the attention of politicians and the general public in Canada; but because the debate has been monopolized by political parties that either have or covet control of the state, the issue is discussed mostly in terms of the exercise and division of power rather than as a social issue in its own right.

Before embarking on that debate, it will be necessary to consider what the relationship of civil and political society with the state actually is. We can be brief about contemporary socialist countries, where, quite simply, the state has appropriated all civil and political life. To put it bluntly, the expression and discussion of alternative social projects is not tolerated. The debate between Marx and Bakounin was settled a long time ago, and statism carried the day (though it is true that the alternative proposed then was anarchism); so the challenge for socialism is to find a better alternative.

In capitalist societies, the question is more complex. At first glance, one would think that more choice is permitted; and yet no one really believes that there is much real choice any more when it comes to political candidates. As we've mentioned, in liberal democracies everywhere, fewer and fewer people have been turning out to vote at elections. Less than twenty-five per cent of the American electorate were enough to put Reagan in office in 1980, and during the 1980 Canadian federal election the underlying issue, as one journalist quipped, was whether or not Canadians have the right to change their government. (Recently, the high turn-outs recorded for the 1983 Chicago election, in which the city elected its first black mayor, and in the provincial election in British Columbia may represent a reversal of this trend, at least where local issues prevail.)

With the Liberals behaving like the rulers of Canada by divine right, and with such narrow ideological distance between the three main parties, choice has indeed been reduced to a minimum. Moreover, as a result of industrialization and advancing urbanization, even small towns and rural communities are affected by the erosion of political society and civil society. Popular culture is under pressure from the state and its institutions.

André Gorz, the French journalist and philosopher, writes in *Ecology as Politics*:

> The rift between production and consumption, between work and "leisure" is the result of the destruction of autonomous human capabilities in favour of the capitalist division of labour. The rift enables the sphere of commodity relations to be perpetuated and indefinitely extended. Having been deprived of all possibility of control over the nature or purpose of labour, the realm of freedom becomes exclusively that of non-work periods. But since all creative or productive activity of any social consequence is nevertheless denied during "free" time, this freedom is itself reduced to a choice amongst objects of consumption and passive entertainment.

Gorz then traces how it is that the destruction of autonomy begins at school, when children are introduced to the specialization of knowledge. If one understands civil society as "the tissue of social relations which individuals establish between themselves and others in society and which do not owe their existence to the intervention or institutional activity of the state," we can see how the autonomization of individuals in society, the isolation and separation of people within an environment rampant with bureaucracy and multiplying dependencies, has helped to undermine civil life. Compartmentalization being one of the key principles of capitalist society — the division of labour, the separation of production and consumption, the nuclear family, apartment blocks and automobiles — individuals are constantly being removed from the collective.

As a method of organization this has had its triumphs, but mainly for the organizers, not for those being organized, and not without terrible disjunctions: the yawning gap between real and ideal, between needs and desires and, of course, between rich and poor. Since the Sixties, these have been present and obvious in everyday life: in the decline of the family and the deterioration of health care systems, education and justice. And always at the bottom, at the end, stands the

lone individual, the pride of liberal society, alone before the
state and the law.

On this subject Rosanvallon writes:

> The power of the state has only one meaning when
> it is exerted on the individual *subject*, and not on
> groups that may have a certain autonomy from the
> state.... In helping to free the individual from
> dependence and reliance on others, the state super-
> vises the autonomization [or individualization] of
> society by which it needs to exist. By reaffirming
> the individual as a self-sufficient entity, the state
> profits from the cultural mutation that it has itself
> accelerated and may even have provoked; for the
> detachment of politics from religion also implies the
> separation of individuals from intermediary social
> groups. In this way, it prepares the *market society*,
> to which its own existence is linked.

As for political society, where the citizens engage in the
discussion of their choices for their society, political parties
and the state have taken over; which is to say that those who
make the decisions today have a vested interest in the
conservation of power and therefore favour debates and
programs that will maximize electoral profits.

So we get the publicity and propaganda approach to
politics; the seduction of consumer-voters rather than the
expression or discussion of important political choice. Absurd
amounts of money are spent on election campaigns nowadays,
despite legislation to control expenditures, legislation that
instead of limiting spending, really only tries to even up the
odds so it doesn't look as if elections can be bought outright.
Opinion polls and ritualized general elections every four or
five years are all that remain of "participatory democracy." If
you don't like the way he's running the store, Trudeau tells us
with a shrug, turf him out at the next election.

Vestigial democracy is what we have under capitalism, and
the illusion there is of more choice than under socialism. The
main difference is that some capitalist societies do not absolutely
forbid the freedom to dissent. Some—South Korea, Taiwan
and Singapore, for example—most emphatically do.

If this long reflection about Canada and Quebec has taken us
through many detours and dredged up a disparate-seeming
batch of ideas for examination, it has nevertheless revealed a

pattern that can be understood as political, yet touching on our personal lives. We have taken the broad perspective, but at the same time started with ourselves and our own lives.

Dumont maintains that the hope for genuine cultural development lies with popular culture and the careful tending of the cultural dimension of daily life. Cultural development begins at home, and so should political and economic regeneration. For how are people who have always yielded their autonomy to others to conceive of national autonomy if they don't begin with themselves and their own immediate communities? Instead of summoning in the experts—Senator Forsey or the Conference Board—to tell us what to think about domination and dependence, we have to come up with our own answers.

While we can take heart at the knowledge that all kinds of people are resisting, we do have to be wary of the solutions being offered. The massive intrusion of the state into our collective lives, often pre-empting genuine collective activity, has, for instance, fuelled the movements of the new Right, which call for a reaffirmation of good old free enterprise and the curtailment of the hated bureaucracy. Under Reaganomics the axe falls on social services; day care and rape crisis centres are expendable but security and defence budgets are not. While asking for freedom from the government in one area of social endeavour—business—neo-conservatives actually want *more* state control in others. However distasteful, the move to the right still has to be seen as a symptom of the social malaise we are experiencing as a civilization.

So far we have spoken rather vaguely about popular culture and the prospects for its revitalization. To give popular culture some shape, we have defined it in opposition to higher-profile mass and élite culture, as the fluid, casual interaction of daily human existence that picks up, as it were, where formalized cultural activity leaves off. It is the cultural values and habits we carry around in our heads and express in our passions and prejudices. It involves everyone—kids, connoisseurs, cops and hockey players.

We have also remarked on the fact that this rich store of ideas, images and stories acts as a creative tributary to mass and élite culture. However, the relationship is not that simple or direct.

Popular culture not only contributes to the general social environment, it is shaped by it. For example, we are all affected by the fact that as a society we have become infatuated with moving pictures and spend huge amounts of time glued to the TV set. We treat television as our main source of information and diversion, without recognizing the qualitative effects of presenting information as entertainment and vice versa. No one can actually specify the relationship between violence in real life and violence on TV.

Finally, we have talked about the deterioration of popular culture in terms of the displacement of customs, the surrender of skills once commonly held and the detachment of politics from daily life. We have allowed all this to go on for so long that the governing process now depends on it; thanks to the relentless march of economic development, we have slowly given up control over leisure time and entertainment as well as over work and education. We live in a world of greed, in a universe of "needs." New products appear daily to gratify needs we never knew we had. Normal bodily functions are classified as "problems," and we are gulled into adopting all manner of inessentials as real necessities (electric toothbrushes, scented toilet paper), paying for the privilege of keeping the wheels of consumerism going.

All societies can be judged by the type of information they value, and by the same token, by the type of information they denigrate. Our society fervently believes in what can be measured and quantified; data that the French economist (and chief adviser to President Mitterrand) Jacques Attali has noted are of the very poorest quality. This information is on a par with the signal, which only acquires value when it elicits a response. "In this vision of the world, information is important, but no more important than a traffic light." More complex forms of information, such as language or mathematics (organized according to a code and translating into a precise meaning) and symbolic or semilogic information (which carries extra meaning along with the literal message, such as figures of speech), curiously enough have nothing like the status and authority of cybernetic data and statistics. In short, the information prized by our civilization emphasizes money and machines and bespeaks the social imagination of a people narrowly oriented toward growth and development—people with no time to pause to smell the flowers.

If we were to imagine another world where a robust and expansive popular culture flourished, it would surely be integrated; it would give room to the subjective, avoiding the trap of socialism's flat denial of the individual on the one hand and liberalism's flat denial of the collective on the other.

Instead of assigning citizens seats on the sidelines, it would demand effort, involvement and imaginative support from everyone, on the assumption that healthy growth will flow from individual intelligence and experience combining to create the collective imagination. Without this respect for the individual and the awakening possibilities for redesigning our home, we might as well throw in the towel, espouse the visions of Peter Lougheed and Bill Davis, and take another Pepin-Robarts committee 'round the mulberry bush.

A well-functioning popular culture would also enjoy a very different relationship with nature, which would be treated at all times as a treasure borrowed from the next generation, and regarded as a responsibility rather than a possession. Private industry and government would then be accountable to the rest of us for any rearranging they do of our environment. They would have to develop a completely different set of attitudes, presenting economic policies with cultural impact studies attached. New projects, especially those entailing introduction of technological innovation, would be expected to justify themselves culturally as well as financially.

And finally, a strong popular culture would belong to a society where the citizens would go a good distance beyond merely retrieving musty old scrolls from the one-time mother country in order to recoup their self-determination. *Autogestion* or self-management would become the main social project and guiding principle, operating on the same level as capitalism and socialism do today.

A great many of the most dynamic though disadvantaged elements of our culture — women, young people, natives, artists — already figure there may be less risk in radical change than in *not* changing and standing passively by. These people cannot help but believe that things could be better for them, as they are demonstrably better for most other people they see around them (and on TV). This is not to deny our manifold blessings in a violent and hungry world. On the contrary, it is because we are comparatively well off that we can and should embark on a major social overhaul.

Surely now is no time to stop asking questions. Granted, some might say that in perilous times we should put our confidence in the system; when the machine starts breaking down, we should all fall behind the authorities so as not to allow the enemy to profit from our internal division. On the other hand, if things are going well, these same people usually spurn objections, accusing the dissenters of ingratitude when "things have never been better." In other words, according to a certain school of thought, the time will never be right.

And why should anyone imagine that only the disinherited and downtrodden have a right to demand large-scale social change, or that *need* and not *desire* should be the only suitable motivation? Certainly the protest movements of recent times have not taken means tests. They have sprouted like mushrooms in all terrains and, as we have remarked, for all the sundry issues they address, they yet display a striking similarity of intent: scepticism about authorities and the accuracy and "objectivity" of official information; a reluctance to take their word for it, especially as it has been shown in the past to be untrustworthy; and a rejection of their monopoly of information.

It was Hegel who once said that if the imagination is revolutionized, reality cannot hold out for long. But if we can no longer determine where to go by consulting the great philosophers, if we can see that the economic and technological imperative driving American imperialism serves only to make individuals superfluous, to turn populations into carbon copies of each other, then we ourselves will have to take over the imagining.

Every society, every culture inculcates its members with an ideal of the good life. Today the mass media diffuse an unrelenting barrage of conscious and subliminal messages that work on people's perceptions — which is why they are so aptly called the consciousness industries, and why they might more aptly be called subconsciousness industries. In portraying society and its values, these industries nourish the social imagination, helping to set the limits of the collective dream.

Now, if imagination is something all people enjoy, we can expect the dreams to vary with the individual and the situation. As with other manifestations of social character, the imagination is situated and dated; ideals are not exempt from change. So the vaunted golden age may be the present lived, the past glorified or the future idealized, depending on the culture. Among other things, the social imagination keeps redefining what is desirable and undesirable, what is probable and improbable, likely and unlikely, possible and impossible. To us, the possible is by far the most important and certainly the most laden with meaning, for while its roots reach into reality, its branches reach toward something new.

The great achievement of capitalist culture has been alienation and heteronomy, which have turned people into hordes of inert, molecular consumers, voters, spectators and users. Civil and political society has been absorbed into a universe of personal objects and private pursuits, which also channel individual and collective desires. So today one of the most revolutionary things citizens can do is to dream about new possibilities.

Dreaming — not daydreaming, but dreaming — about a different future for Quebec and Canada is the first step. Insisting that those affected by a decision be consulted and involved in the decision is the second. All it requires is some optimism and a willingness to think the heretofore unthinkable. And a conviction that a wholesale reordering really is feasible. We have already started converting from the consumer society to the conserver society. Why stop there? Looking about us, we see people are no longer blindly accepting the idea that money can buy answers, that science is infallible and will always find a way, or that big organizations can do things better than small ones.

Because we love our countries and believe in our fellow citizens, we feel confident that we will find the fresh solutions we so badly need. Unlike some English Canadians who doubt that Canada can exist as a nation without Quebec, we are convinced that English Canada exists, as does Canadian culture, distinct and independent of American or British or Québécois culture and wants only the room and recognition to flourish. Canada has undergone an unprecedented cultural awakening of late, and throughout the country, all kinds of people have realized that the nether side of economic dependence is cultural vassalage, which reaches into the souls of people. It is the terminal stage of imperialism.

Yet the crisis we are going through has already helped many Canadians regain confidence in their heritage, and this has led them to pay special attention to the creators in their communities, to the traditions and values native to their place. In both Canada and Quebec, the road toward national liberation and autonomy has been broached, and it appears more and more that Canada is engaged in the same search as Quebec is. If there are Canadians today who have stopped fearing the thought of an independent Quebec, and have come to hold the same hope for their own nation, they may also have come to understand that when Quebeckers say "yes" to Quebec (as forty per cent of them did in the referendum), they are not necessarily saying "no" to Canada. Quite the opposite, they may be saying "yes" to a new and better relationship.

Here is the quintessential ambiguity of the Quebec situation. If Quebeckers harboured only spite and dislike for Canadians, they would probably have left long ago. It is because they have affection and esteem for Canada and Canadians that the majority are still reluctant to sever old ties. While wanting more autonomy, if not sovereignty, most Quebeckers are still ready to delegate the power of their sovereignty to federal institutions, especially those running economic affairs. And perhaps these Quebeckers have something in common with these Canadian "mappists" who take refuge in their mythic territorial expanse. As far as we know, neither the Rockies that Jean Chrétien and Mme. Chaput-Rolland weep tears for, nor the rustic Quebec some English Canadians wax sentimental about, will disappear, even if it were to happen that Quebec and Canada recognized each other as sovereign countries some day.

Instead of the suspicion and disdain sown by fanatics on both sides, under a new association our two peoples could well develop a completely new relationship based on self-confidence and solidarity.

We were not persuaded, however, that much would ever come of constitutional horse-trading by the premiers and provincial attorneys-general in hotel kitchens, or of charters of rights made over the heads of the citizens. Once the dust settled after the referendum, it was very clear that the majority of Quebeckers had voted for profound change, regardless of whether they voted for sovereignty–association or renewed federalism. But change is the last thing the federal forces claiming victory had in mind. So far as Canada is concerned, The Question has been settled, and the constitution has been retrieved. Provincial premiers are anxious to get on with their bickering over resource ownership, and the Progressive Conservatives wanted to get back to their leader-slaying rituals. Thus pontificated Premier Davis to his fellow Canadians on Dominion Day in 1980: "Canadians are on the verge of finding harmony."

Where this "harmony" will lead is uncertain, but the continued stasis of two national majorities is likely. If there are Canadians who have resented Ottawa's preoccupation with Quebec and seen Quebec's demands as an impediment to their own, they have had cause. The irony is that many Quebeckers looking at the same situation have read it as Ottawa rejecting Quebec nationalism in favour of Canadian nationalism. The truth is that Ottawa has been playing off one nationalism against the other and has no intention of satisfying either. Instead of resolving anything, the two protagonists have merely been paralysed.

It seems to us that we have to look to other sources of strength and ingenuity if we are to negotiate our way out of the web of crises. And to bring about the renewal of our two nations, we will have to take into account the whole assembly of troubles — including American imperialism — afflicting our societies, and look beyond to the larger problems inherent in capitalist and socialist societies generally. Those who proclaim themselves realists and put their stock in a reality that can be measured and controlled will tend to disparage discussing "soft" issues such as culture, but where has all the talk about inflation, unemployment and supply-side economics taken us so far? What has loyalty to the "practical" and the realistic done for humankind lately? And haven't we put off, for far too long, paying heed to the "immaterial," which is to say the valuative and imaginative side of life, which only an age such as ours would use as a synonym for "unimportant"?

It is time for Canadians and Quebeckers to stop imitating the empire, to take an honest look together at our relations with the United States and the rest of the world and at our achievements as two societies and resolve to reinvent the future and repatriate our souls.

Sources

Following is a partial list of sources, including all those cited in the text. They are listed by page number.

Introduction

7   Fromm, Erich. *Escape from Freedom* (New York: Holt Rinehart & Winston, 1965).

Chapter 1: Deux Pays pour Vivre

11   Rotstein, Abraham. "Is There an English-Canadian Nationalism?" *Journal of Canadian Studies*, Summer 1978.

12   Watkins, Melville. "Coming Apart Together," *This Magazine*, May/June 1979.

19   Grant, George. *Lament for a Nation* (Toronto: Carleton Library, 1970).

20   Grant, *Lament*, p. 41.

Chapter 2: In the Shadow of American Imperialism

25   Morton, W.L. *The Canadian Identity* (University of Toronto Press, 1972).

31-32   Cordell, Arthur J. *The Multinational Firm, Foreign Direct Investment and Canadian Science Policy* (Ottawa: Science Council of Canada, 1971).

32   Levitt, Kari. *Silent Surrender* (Toronto: Macmillan, 1970).

33   Donner, Arthur. *Financing the Future: Canada's Capital Markets in the Eighties* (Toronto: James Lorimer/Canadian Institute for Economic Policy, 1982), p. 157.

34   Powrie, T.L. "The Contribution of Foreign Capital to Canadian Economic Growth" (unpublished paper, 1977).

36-37   United States Senate. *Implications of Multinational Firms for World Trade and Investment and for US Trade and Labor* (Washington: Committee on Finance, Russell B. Long, Chairman, 1973).

37   US Senate, *Implications*, p. 612.

37   Gray, Herb. *Foreign Direct Investment in Canada* (Ottawa: Government of Canada, 1972).

38   Grant, George. *Technology and Empire* (Toronto: Anansi, 1969).

38   Marcuse, Herbert. *One Dimensional Man* (Boston: Beacon Press, 1964).

39   US Senate, *Implications*, p. 49.

39   Levitt, Kari. "Canada: Economic Dependence and Political Disintegration," *New World Quarterly* 4, no. 2 (1968): 113.

40-41   Quoted in Levitt, "Economic Dependence," p. 110.

41-42   Watkins, Melville. "The Regulation of Multinationals and Foreign Direct Investment" (unpublished paper, 1979).

44   Canada, House of Commons. Committee on Defence. *Minutes of Proceedings and Evidence.* 22 October 1963, p. 510.

44   Kent, Tom. "The Changing Place of Canada," *Foreign Affairs* 35 (July 1957): 581.

44   Minifie, James M. *Peacemaker or Powder-Monkey:*

Canada's Role in a Revolutionary World (Toronto: McClelland and Stewart, 1960).

46 Doyle, Kevin. "Free Trade Looms," *Report on Confederation*, March 1980.

47-48 Britton, John and James Gilmour. *The Weakest Link* (Ottawa: Science Council of Canada, 1978), pp. 22-23.

49 Quoted in Watkins, "Regulation of Multinationals."

50 Royal Commission on National Development in the Arts, Letters and Sciences, *Report* (Ottawa: 1951), p. 13.

50 Audley, Paul. *Canada's Cultural Industries* (Toronto: James Lorimer/Canadian Institute for Economic Policy, 1983).

50 Clarkson, Stephen. *Canada and the Reagan Challenge* (Toronto: James Lorimer/Canadian Institute for Economic Policy, 1982).

52 Bureau of Management Consulting. *The Film Industry in Canada* (Ottawa: Secretary of State, 1976).

54-55 Hardin, Herschel. *A Nation Unaware* (Vancouver: J.J. Douglas, 1974), p. 54.

56 Escarpit, Robert. *The Book Revolution* (Paris: UNESCO, 1966), p. 91.

56 Porter, John. *The Vertical Mosaic* (Toronto: University of Toronto Press, 1965).

56 Clement, Wallace. *The Canadian Corporate Elite* (Toronto: McClelland and Stewart, 1975).

61-62 Monière, Denis. *Le Développement des idéologies au Québec* (Montréal: Québec/Amérique, 1977).

63 Dumont, Fernand. *The Vigil of Quebec* (Toronto: University of Toronto Press, 1974), p. xiii.

68-69 Melnyk, George. *Radical Regionalism* (Edmonton: NeWest Press, 1981).

69 Frye, Northrop. "Conference Summary," *Options* (Toronto: Media Centre, University of Toronto, 1977), p. 439.

70   Breton, Albert. "Minority Comment," *Report of the Federal Cultural Policy Review Committee* (Ottawa: 1982), p. 362.

70-71   _____. *Report*, pp. 4, 6.

71-72   Meisel, John. "Five Steps to Survival." Gerstein Lectures, York University, Toronto, 10 April 1981.

72   Frazee, Rowland C. "Best Friends—Whether We Like It or Not," *Chimo,* April 1983.

Chapter 3: Culture and Empire

75   Castoriadis, Cornelius, quoted in Dick Howard, "Notes and Commentary," *Telos,* no 23 (Spring 1975), p. 123.

76-77   "Tribunale de la Culture," *Liberté,* no. 101 (vol. 17, no.5): 30-31.

77   Ostry, Bernard. *The Cultural Connection* (Toronto: McClelland and Stewart, 1978).

78   Federal Cultural Policy Review Committee. *Speaking of our Culture* (Ottawa: 1980).

81   Lenin, V. I. *Collected Works* (Moscow: Foreign Languages Publishing House, 1960) 27: 339, 350.

83   Leontieff, Vassily. *The Future of World Economy* (Cambridge: Oxford University Press, 1979).

83   Heilbroner, Robert. *Business and Civilization in Decline* (New York: Norton, 1977).

94-95   "Tribunale," pp. 37, 38, 39.

98   Symons, T.H.B. *To Know Ourselves.* Report of the Commission on Canadian Studies (Ottawa: Association of Universities and Colleges of Canada, 1975), 2 vols., p. 133.

98-99   Quoted by Richard Gwyn, "Canadian Universities Fail an Examination," *Toronto Star,* 9 March 1976.

9   Page, James E. *Reflections on the Symons Report: The State of Canadian Studies in 1980* (Ottawa: Secretary of State, 1981).

99   Fanon, Frantz. *Black Skins, White Masks* (New York: Grove Press, 1967).

100   Williams, Raymond. *Television, Technology and Cultural Form* (Glasgow: Fontana, 1974).

101   Williams, *Television, p. 42.*

103   Bell, Daniel. *The End of Ideology* (New York: Free Press, 1966).

104   Lévy-Leblond, J.M. and A. Joubert. *(Auto) critique de la science* (Paris: Seuil, 1975), p. 3.

104   Lévy-Leblond and Joubert, *(Auto)critique,* p. 109.

105   Dickson, David. *The Politics of Alternative Technology* (New York: Universe Books, 1975), p. 16.

105-06   Castoriadis, Cornelius. *Encyclopaedia Universalis* (Paris: 1968) 15:806.

106   Williams, *Television,* pp. 127-28.

107   Brecht, Bertolt. *Theory of Radio,* vol. 3 (Frankfurt: aM. Suhrkamp, 1967).

107   Enzensberger, Hans Magnus. *The Consciousness Industry* (New York: Seabury Press, 1974), p. 96.

108   Baudrillard, Jean. *Pour une critique de l'économie politique de signe* (Paris: Gallimard, 1973), p. 210.

112   Mattelart, Armand and Michèle Mattelart. *De l'usage des médias* (Paris: Alain Moreau, 1979).

112-13   Schiller, Herbert I. *Who Knows: Information in the Age of the Fortune 500* (Norwood, N.J.: Ablex Publishing, 1981).

           _____. *Communication and Cultural Domination* (White Plains, N.Y.: IASP, 1976).

           _____. *Mass Communication and American Empire* (Boston: Beacon Press, 1969).

114   Brzezinski, Zbigniew. *Between Two Ages: America's Role in the Technetronic Age* (New York: Viking, 1970), p. 305.

115   Luce, Henry R. *The American Century* (New York: Farrar and Rinehart, 1941), p. 23.

116   Guback, Thomas H. *The International Film Industry:*

Western Europe and America since 1945 (Blooming-ton, Ind.: Indiana University Press, 1969).

117 Mattelart, Armand and Michèle Mattelart, "Une culture pour gérer la crise," *Le Monde diplomatique,* October 1979.

121 Osolnik, Bogdan. *Aims and Approaches to a New International Communications Order.* Prepared for the third session of the International Commission for the Study of Communications Problems, July 1978 (Paris: UNESCO).

121 Berque, Jacques. *La Dépossession du monde* (Paris: Seuil, 1964).

122 Nora, Simon and Alain Minc. *L'Informatisation de la société* (Paris: Documentation Française, 1978), pp. 63, 115.

122 Brzezinski, *Between Two Ages,* pp. 24, 32.

124 Lodge, George. *The New American Ideology* (New York: Knopf, 1974), p. 3.

124 Bell, Daniel. *The Cultural Contradictions of Capitalism* (New York: Basic Books, 1976), p. 53.

124-25 Toffler, Alvin. *The Third Wave* (New York: William Morrow, 1980), p. 281.

125 Toffler, *Third Wave,* p. 167.

128 Castoriadis, Cornelius. "Transformation sociale et création culturelle," *Sociologie et sociétés* 11, no. 1 (April 1979): 33.

Chapter 4: Reinventing the Future

129-30 UNESCO, *Cultural Rights as Human Rights.* Studies and Documents in Cultural Policies, no. 3 (Paris: 1970).

131 McPhail, Thomas L. *Electronic Colonialism* (Beverly Hills/London: Sage Publications, 1981).

133 Dumont, Fernand. "L'idée de développement culturel: esquisse pour une psychanalyse," *Sociologie et sociétés* 11, no.1 (April 1979).

134   Dumont, "Développement culturel," p. 24.

134   Frye, Northrop. *Divisions on a Ground* (Toronto: Anansi, 1982), p. 62.

135   Hearn, Francis. *Domination, Legitimation and Resistance* (Westport, Conn.: Greenwood Press, 1978).

136   Dumont, "Développement culturel," p. 28.

136-37   Brecht, Bertolt. *Écrits sur le théâtre* (Paris: Arche, 1972).

137   Salutin, Rick. "The Culture Vulture," *This Magazine*, December 1978.

138   Resnick, Philip. *The Land of Cain* (Vancouver: New Star, 1977), p. 167.

139   Moore, Steve and Debi Wells. "The Myth of Canadian Deindustrialization" in *Imperialism, Nationalism and Canada* (Toronto: New Hogtown Press, 1977).

139-40   Hutcheson, John. *Dominance and Dependency* (Toronto: McClelland and Stewart, 1978).

140   Task Force on Canadian Unity, *A Future Together: Observations and Recommendations* (Ottawa: 1977), p. 118.

141   Kostash, Myrna. *Long Way From Home* (Toronto: James Lorimer, 1980), p. 247.

142   Quoted in *Rapport de la Commission d'enquête sur l'enseignement des arts* (Éditeur officiel du Québec, 1969), vol. 1, p. 38.

143   Bahro, Rudolf. *L'Alternative* (Paris: Stock, 1979).

143   Marcuse, Herbert. "Protosocialisme et le capitalisme avancé," *Les temps modernes*, no. 384 (March 1979): 1714.

148   Rosanvallon, Pierre. *Le Capitalisme utopique* (Paris: Seuil, 1979), p. 107.

149   Rosanvallon, *Capitalisme*, p. 230.

149-50   Rosanvallon, *Capitalisme*, p. 229.

151   Gorz, André. *Ecology as Politics* (Montreal: Black Rose, 1980), p. 34.

152   Rosanvallon, *Capitalisme,* p. 86.

154   Attali, Jacques. *La Parole et l'outil* (Paris: PF, 1975), p. 73.

Also from James Lorimer & Company

QUEBEC IN QUESTION
Marcel Rioux

Quebec in Question traces the history of Quebec from Champlain to Lévesque from the viewpoint of an advocate of independence. This lucid and scholarly book is the best introduction available for English-language readers to the intellectual foundations of the independence movement.

QUEBEC: A HISTORY 1867–1929
Paul-André Linteau, René Durocher and Jean-Claude Robert

This ambitious work by three major Quebec historians describes the period that saw Quebec transformed from a rural society into an industrial one. The text of this widely acclaimed book is complemented by 190 photographs, 15 maps and 60 tables and graphs.

THE ASBESTOS STRIKE
Edited by Pierre E. Trudeau

Pierre Elliott Trudeau first came to prominence with this classic study of the 1949 Asbestos strike, in which the miners were pitted against both the company and the Duplessis government.

RUMOURS OF WAR
Ron Haggart and Aubrey E. Golden

This classic study of the 1970 October Crisis focuses on the logic of the widespread arrests of political activists, their internments and interrogations.

HOW LÉVESQUE WON
Pierre Dupont

The story behind the collapse of the Bourassa government and René Lévesque's election campaign leading to the dramatic Parti Québécois victory on November 15, 1976.

WHAT DOES QUEBEC WANT?
André Bernard

Written specifically for an English-Canadian audience, this book examines both historical precedent and current attitudes to show that French-speaking Québécois share a body of important beliefs and goals that transcend their partisan differences.

THE ARROW
James Dow

When the Diefenbaker government scrapped the Arrow, a Canadian supersonic fighter, in 1959, many saw it as symbolic of Canada's inability to emerge from the shadows of the UK and the US. Working from a wide range of sources, James Dow reconstructs this remarkable chapter in Canadian history.

CANADA AND THE REAGAN CHALLENGE
Crisis in the Canadian-American Relationship
Stephen Clarkson

In this widely acclaimed study, Stephen Clarkson focuses on the crisis of 1981, when the new nationalism of the federal Liberal government ran head-on into the "America-first" foreign policy of the US Reagan administration. US control of the Canadian economy was at the centre of the conflict, but Clarkson reviews as well the other major issues in the bilateral relationship: trade barriers and incentives, NATO and NORAD, acid rain, the fisheries, and cultural and communications policies.

CANADA'S CULTURAL INDUSTRIES
Broadcasting, Publishing, Records and Film
Paul Audley

For both English and French Canada, Paul Audley provides a wealth of information on the state of the cultural industries: newspapers, magazines, books, recording, radio, television and film. Audley pays particular attention to problems of Canadian content and control, and how government could formulate new policies to strengthen these vital industries.

LONG WAY FROM HOME
The Story of the Sixties Generation in Canada
Myrna Kostash

In this unique study of the Sixties in Canada, Myrna Kostash focuses on the political involvement of students in the peace and anti-nuclear movements, the counterculture, the rebirth of feminism, Quebec nationalism, "red power" and the struggle to Canadianize universities.